EXPLORING SPANISH

GRADES 1-2

D1214734

AMERICAN
EDUCATION
PUBLISHING™

An imprint of Carson-Dellosa Publishing
Greensboro, NC

American Education Publishing™
An imprint of Carson-Dellosa Publishing LLC
P.O. Box 35665
Greensboro, NC 27425 USA

ISBN 978-1-60996-786-4

8711

TABLE OF CONTENTS

uno

dos

tres

cuatro

cinco

seis

siete

ocho

nueve

diez

Numbers 1–5

Say each word out loud.

uno  1

dos  2

tres  3

cuatro  4

cinco  5

Numbers Review

Write the number next to the Spanish word. Circle the correct number of animals for each number shown. Then, color the pictures.

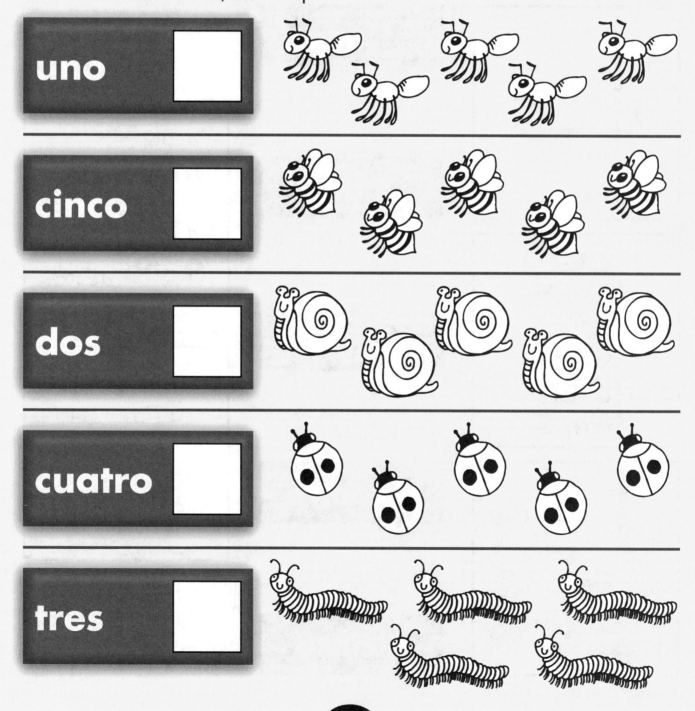

uno

cinco

dos

cuatro

tres

Matching Numbers

Draw a line from the word to the correct picture. Then, color the pictures.

1 uno

2 dos

3 tres

4 cuatro

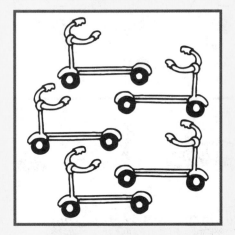

5 cinco

Matching 1–10

Draw a line to match each object to the number that is written in Spanish.

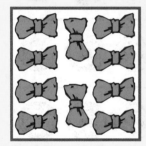

uno	1
dos	2
tres	3
cuatro	4
cinco	5
seis	6
siete	7
ocho	8
nueve	9
diez	10

Count the Cookies

In each box at the left, write the number that matches the Spanish word. Cross out the correct number of cookies to show the number written in Spanish. The first one is done for you.

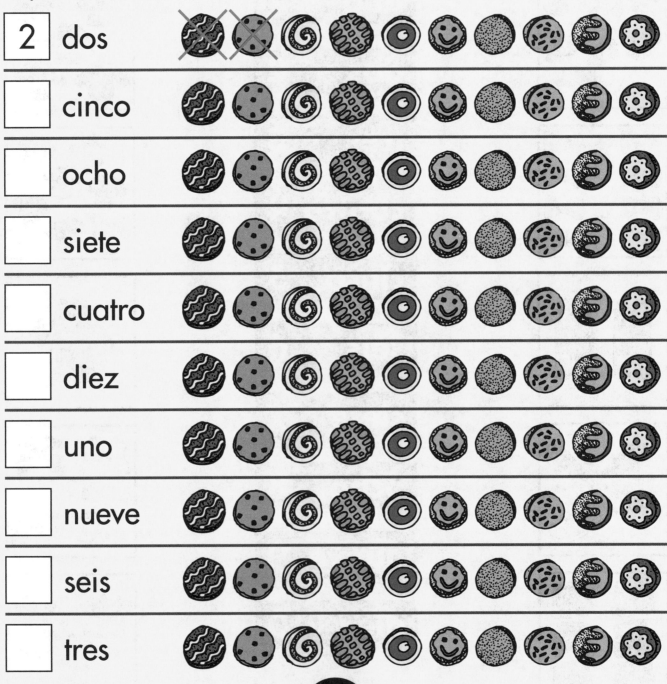

2	dos	
	cinco	
	ocho	
	siete	
	cuatro	
	diez	
	uno	
	nueve	
	seis	
	tres	

My Favorite Number

Write your favorite number from 1 to 10 in the boxes. Draw a picture to show that number.

My favorite number is ☐.

In Spanish, it is called ☐.

Circles 1-10

Draw the correct number of circles in each box.

uno		seis	
dos		siete	
tres		ocho	
cuatro		nueve	
cinco		diez	

Numbers 0–10

Trace, then write each of the number words from 0 to 10 in Spanish.
Use the words at the left to help you.

0	cero	cero
1	uno	uno
2	dos	dos
3	tres	tres
4	cuatro	cuatro
5	cinco	cinco
6	seis	seis
7	siete	siete
8	ocho	ocho
9	nueve	nueve
10	diez	diez

Dot-to-Dot

Connect the dots. Start with the Spanish word for **one** and stop at **ten**.

What shape do you see? _____

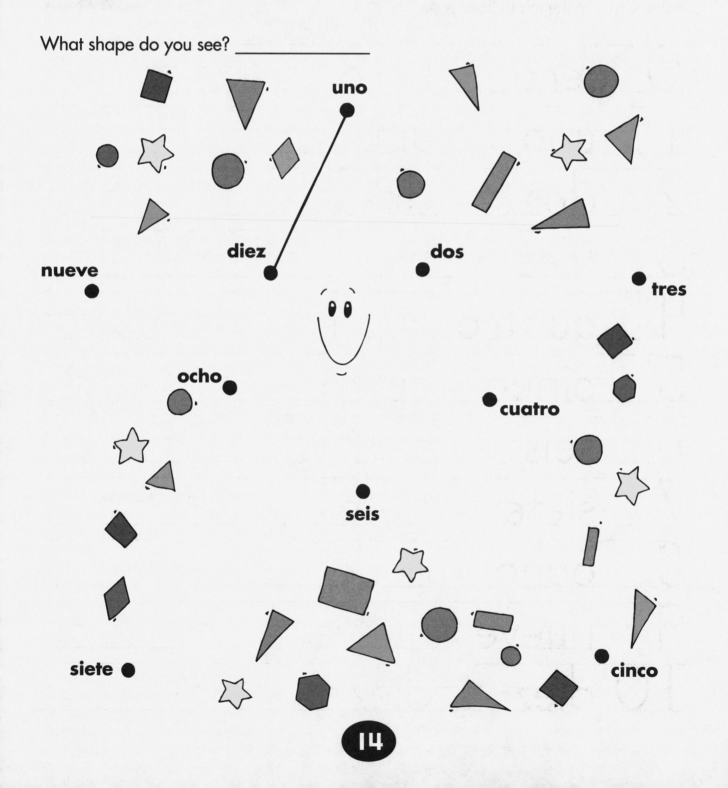

Numbers 0–20

In the left column, write the number words from 0 to 10 in Spanish. Use the words in the box below to help you. Then, in the second column, write the numbers beside each Spanish word. Two are done for you.

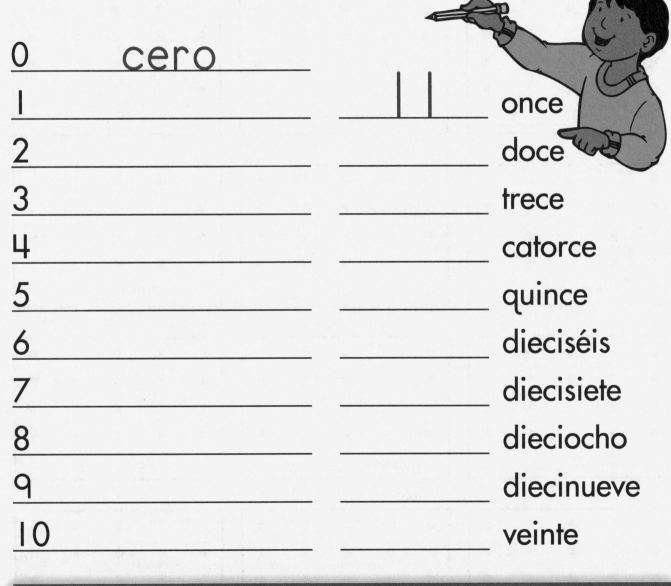

0   cero

1   once

2   doce

3   trece

4   catorce

5   quince

6   dieciséis

7   diecisiete

8   dieciocho

9   diecinueve

10   veinte

siete	uno	nueve	cinco	cuatro	tres
ocho	seis	cero	dos	diez	

Sunshine 0–20

Write the number for each Spanish word. Cross out the correct number of suns to show the number written in Spanish. The first one is done for you.

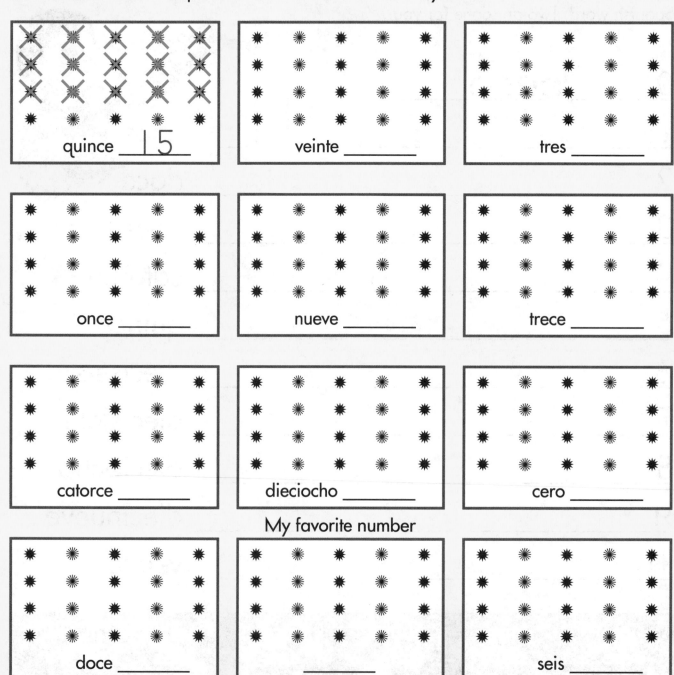

quince __15__

veinte _____

tres _____

once _____

nueve _____

trece _____

catorce _____

dieciocho _____

cero _____

My favorite number

doce _____

_____

seis _____

Numbers Crossword

Write the Spanish number words in the puzzle spaces. Use the words at the bottom to help you.

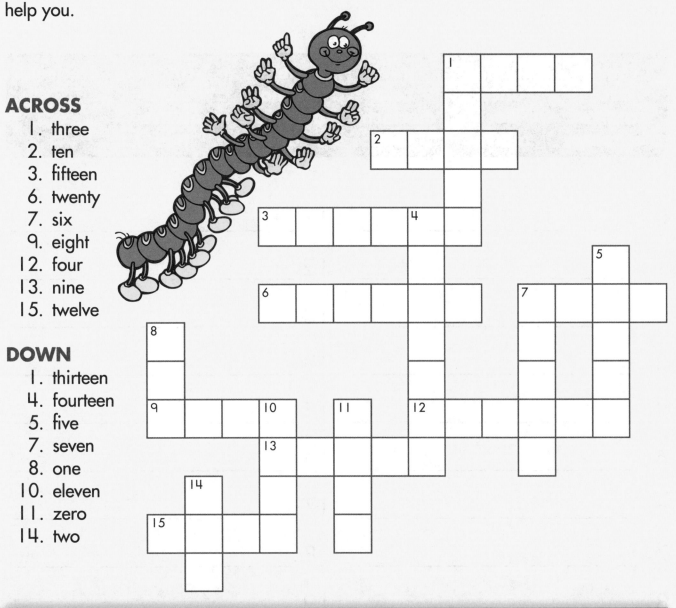

ACROSS
1. three
2. ten
3. fifteen
6. twenty
7. six
9. eight
12. four
13. nine
15. twelve

DOWN
1. thirteen
4. fourteen
5. five
7. seven
8. one
10. eleven
11. zero
14. two

once	doce	veinte	cuatro	ocho	quince
nueve	catorce	cinco	diez	siete	uno
trece	cero	tres	seis	dos	

Numbers

After each numeral, write the number word in Spanish. Use the words below to help you.

veinte	cuatro	trece	siete	cinco	dieciséis
doce	once	cero	ocho	seis	
catorce	dos	dieciocho	diecisiete	quince	
diecinueve	nueve	diez	uno	tres	

0 _____

1 _____

2 _____

3 _____

4 _____

5 _____

6 _____

7 _____

8 _____

9 _____

10 _____

11 _____

12 _____

13 _____

14 _____

15 _____

16 _____

17 _____

18 _____

19 _____

20 _____

Counting On

Follow a pattern to write the numbers from 21–30. Change veinte (20) to veinti and add the number words from uno to nueve. (Watch for accent marks on *dos, tres,* and *seis.*) Rewrite the number words from the word bank in order.

veintiséis	veinticinco	veintisiete	veintinueve	veintiocho
veintidós	veintiuno	treinta	veintitrés	veinticuatro

21 _____   26 _____

22 _____   27 _____

23 _____   28 _____

24 _____   29 _____

25 _____   30 _____

Complete the pattern to write the numbers from 31–39. Use the Spanish word *y* (and) to join *treinta* (30) with the number words *uno* to *nueve*. One is done for you.

31 <u>treinta y uno</u>   36 _____

32 _____   37 _____

33 _____   38 _____

34 _____   39 _____

35 _____

Number Find

Circle the Spanish number words
that you find in the word search.
Then, write the English meaning of
each word. Words can be across,
down, diagonal, or backward.

d	u	e	t	e	i	s	o	d	n	e	e
t	o	a	i	z	l	h	i	u	c	v	t
r	v	c	t	j	c	e	e	a	h	l	e
e	j	e	e	o	c	v	t	u	i	h	i
s	t	p	i	i	e	o	g	n	e	e	s
b	i	r	o	n	r	v	p	q	m	c	i
z	t	c	e	c	t	m	t	c	s	n	t
e	h	a	e	i	c	i	v	h	o	i	n
o	v	p	z	s	n	i	d	e	d	u	i
e	t	n	i	e	v	t	n	ó	c	q	e
s	e	i	s	a	z	o	a	c	s	n	v
v	e	i	n	t	i	u	n	o	o	c	o

Spanish Word	English	Spanish Word	English
doce	_____	siete	_____
catorce	_____	ocho	_____
veintiuno	_____	veintidós	_____
veintisiete	_____	cinco	_____
once	_____	seis	_____
dos	_____	quince	_____
nueve	_____	tres	_____
veinte	_____	dieciocho	_____
treinta	_____		

Counting by Tens

The Spanish numbers ten, twenty, thirty, forty, and fifty are written out of order below. Write the value of each number word in the blank.

_____ treinta   _____ cincuenta   _____ cuarenta

_____ diez   _____ veinte

Write the numbers 30–59 in Spanish. Numbers 41–59 follow the same pattern as numbers 31–39.

30 _____   45 _____

31 _____   46 _____

32 _____   47 _____

33 _____   48 _____

34 _____   49 _____

35 _____   50 _____

36 _____   51 _____

37 _____   52 _____

38 _____   53 _____

39 _____   54 _____

40 _____   55 _____

41 _____   56 _____

42 _____   57 _____

43 _____   58 _____

44 _____   59 _____

Spanish Alphabet

EL ABECEDARIO (EL ALFABETO) EN ESPAÑOL

Aa	a	Jj	jota	Rr	ere
Bb	be	Kk	ka	Ss	ese
Cc	ce	Ll	ele	Tt	te
CHch	che	LLll	elle	Uu	u
Dd	de	Mm	eme	Vv	ve
Ee	e	Nn	ene	Ww	doble ve
Ff	efe	Ññ	eñe	Xx	equis
Gg	ge	Oo	o	Yy	i griega
Hh	hache	Pp	pe	Zz	zeta
Ii	i	Qq	cu		

Rhyming Vowel Practice
Say these sentences out loud:

A, E, I, O, U, ¡Más sabe el burro que tú!

A, E, I, O, U, ¿Cuántos años tienes tú?

Listening Practice

Say the Spanish word for each number out loud.
Write the first letter of the words you hear.

1 _____   4 _____   7 _____

2 _____   5 _____   8 _____

3 _____   6 _____   9 _____

Color the letters of the Spanish alphabet. Say them in Spanish as you color them.

A   B   C   CH   D

E   F   G   H   I

J   K   L   LL   M

N   Ñ   O   P   Q

R   S   T   U   V

W   X   Y   Z

The Alphabet

El abecedario (the alphabet)

a	a	**h**	hache	**ñ**	eñe	**v**	ve
b	be	**i**	i	**o**	o	**w**	doble ve
c	ce	**j**	jota	**p**	pe	**x**	equis
ch	che	**k**	ka	**q**	cu	**y**	i griega
d	de	**l**	ele	**r**	ere	**z**	zeta
e	e	**ll**	elle	**s**	ese		
f	efe	**m**	eme	**t**	te		
g	ge	**n**	ene	**u**	u		

Listening Practice

Write each letter of the alphabet as you say it out loud.

1. _____	7. _____	13. _____	19. _____	25. _____
2. _____	8. _____	14. _____	20. _____	26. _____
3. _____	9. _____	15. _____	21. _____	27. _____
4. _____	10. _____	16. _____	22. _____	28. _____
5. _____	11. _____	17. _____	23. _____	29. _____
6. _____	12. _____	18. _____	24. _____	

you (informal)

tú

usted

you (formal)

pretty

bonita

ugly

feo

happy

alegre

to read

leer

sad

triste

to play

jugar

to eat

comer

Using *You*

Spanish uses two different forms of the pronoun *you*.

Tú is used when talking to

1. someone you refer to by a first name.
2. your sister, brother, or cousin.
3. a classmate.
4. a close friend.
5. a child younger than yourself.

tú

usted

Usted (Ud.) is used when talking to

1. someone with a title.
2. an older person.
3. a stranger.
4. a person of authority.

Write the names of six or more people in each box below.

Use **tú** when you are talking to:	Use **usted** when you are talking to:

Masculine and Feminine

All Spanish nouns and adjectives have gender. This means they are either masculine or feminine. Here are two basic rules to help determine the gender of words. There are other rules for gender that you will learn as you study more Spanish.

1. Spanish words ending in -o are usually masculine.
2. Spanish words ending in -a are usually feminine.

Write the following words in the charts to determine their gender. Write the English meanings to the right. Use a Spanish-English dictionary if you need help.

maestra	ventana	anaranjado	amiga	camisa	queso
amigo	puerta	blanco	falda	chaqueta	tienda
silla	cuaderno	negro	abrigo	sopa	museo
rojo	escritorio	maestro	vestido	fruta	casa

Masculine		Feminine	
words ending in -o	meaning of the word	words ending in -a	meaning of the word

More Than One

Spanish nouns can be placed into two groups—singular nouns (one of something) or plural nouns (more than one of something). Nouns that end in –s are usually plural. Nouns ending in other letters are usually singular.

Read the following familiar nouns. Write **S** if the noun is singular and **P** if the noun is plural.

_____	**1.** calcetines	_____	**5.** dedo	_____	**9.** botas
_____	**2.** cuerpo	_____	**6.** vegetales	_____	**10.** ciudad
_____	**3.** escuela	_____	**7.** sandalias	_____	**11.** zapatos
_____	**4.** guantes	_____	**8.** casa	_____	**12.** boca

Follow these rules to write the following Spanish words in the plural.

1. If the word ends in a vowel, add –s.

2. If the word ends in a consonant, add –es.

3. If the word ends in z, change the z to c before adding –es.

1. carne _____

2. silla _____

3. ciudad _____

4. lápiz _____

5. azul _____

6. nariz _____

7. abrigo _____

8. señor _____

9. borrador _____

10. pollo _____

More and More

Write the plural form of each Spanish clue word in the puzzle.

ACROSS

1. hombro
4. falda
5. zapato
7. museo
8. nariz
10. gato
11. sombrero
13. oso
14. lápiz

DOWN

2. borrador
3. vaso
6. escuela
9. casa
12. mesa

It's a Small World

In Spanish, there are four ways to say "the"—*el, la, los,* and *las*. The definite article (the) agrees with its noun in gender (masculine or feminine) and number (singular or plural).

Masculine singular nouns go with *el*. Feminine singular nouns go with *la*.

Examples: *el libro* (the book)   *el papel* (the paper)
la silla (the chair)   *la regla* (the ruler)

Masculine plural nouns go with *los*. Feminine plural nouns go with *las*.

Examples: *los libros* (the books)   *los papeles* (the papers)
las sillas (the chairs)   *las reglas* (the rulers)

Refer to the word bank to complete the chart. Write the singular and plural forms and the correct definite articles. Two have been done for you.

| cuaderno | mesa | pluma | oso | falda |
| papel | gato | bota | silla | libro |

English	Masculine Singular	Masculine Plural
the book	*el libro*	*los libros*
the paper		
the notebook		
the cat		
the bear		

English	Feminine Singular	Feminine Plural
the chair	*la silla*	*las sillas*
the table		
the boot		
the skirt		
the pen		

One or Some

In English, the words *a*, *an*, and *some* are indefinite articles. In Spanish, there are four indefinite articles—*un*, *una*, *unas*, and *unos*.

Masculine singular nouns go with *un*. Feminine singular nouns go with *una*.

Examples: *un libro* (a book)   *una silla* (a chair)
            un papel (a paper)   *una mesa* (a table)

Masculine plural nouns go with unos. Feminine plural nouns go with unas.

Examples: *unos libros* (some books)   *unas sillas* (some chairs)
            unos papeles (some papers)   *unas mesas* (some tables)

Refer to the word bank to complete the chart. Write the singular and plural forms and the correct indefinite articles. One has been done for you.

| cuaderno | mesa | pluma | oso | falda |
| papel | gato | bota | silla | libro |

English	Masculine Singular	Masculine Plural
a book	un libro	unos libros
a paper		
a notebook		
a cat		
a bear		

English	Feminine Singular	Feminine Plural
a chair		
a table		
a boot		
a skirt		
a pen		

Pretty Colors

Adjectives are words that tell about or describe nouns. Color each box as indicated in Spanish. Use a Spanish-English dictionary if you need help.

rojo	azul	verde	anaranjado	morado

amarillo	café	negro	blanco	rosado

Here are some new adjectives. Copy the Spanish adjectives in the boxes. Write the Spanish words next to the English words at the bottom of the page.

bonita		feo	
	pretty		ugly
grande		pequeño	
	big		small
limpio		sucio	
	clean		dirty
viejo		nuevo	
	old		new
alegre		triste	
	happy		sad

old _____   pretty _____   happy _____

big _____   small _____   ugly _____

new _____   dirty _____

clean _____   sad _____

Words to Describe

Descriptive adjectives are words that describe nouns. Refer to the word bank to write the Spanish adjective that describes each picture.

alegre	alto	sucio	nuevo	abierto	triste	feo	rico
limpio	grande	bajo	bonita	pequeño	cerrado	viejo	pobre

large	new	ugly	happy

old	sad	small	clean

pretty	dirty	tall	open

rich	short	closed	poor

Words to Describe

Write the Spanish words for the clue words in the crossword puzzle.

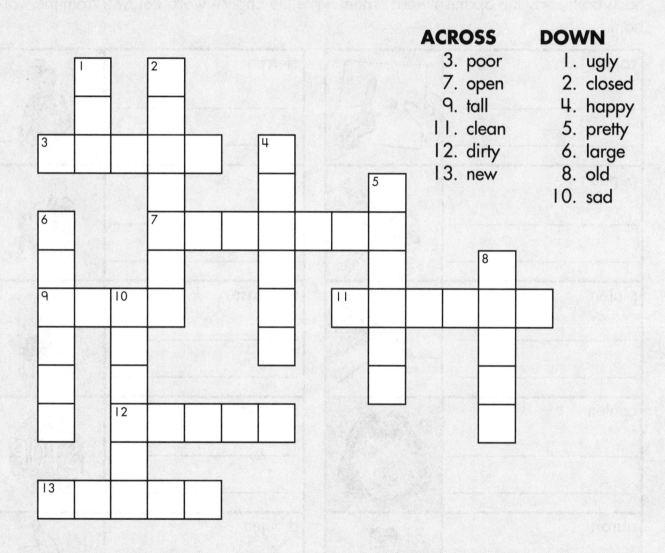

ACROSS
3. poor
7. open
9. tall
11. clean
12. dirty
13. new

DOWN
1. ugly
2. closed
4. happy
5. pretty
6. large
8. old
10. sad

| viejo | bonita | alto | feo | nuevo | cerrado | alegre |
| limpio | abierto | pobre | grande | triste | sucio | |

Open and Close

Would you know what to do if your teacher told you to do something in Spanish? In each box, copy the Spanish word. Then, write the English word below it from the word bank.

corten		cierren	
_____		_____	
_____		_____	
peguen		levántense	
_____		_____	
_____		_____	
pinten		siéntense	
_____		_____	
_____		_____	
canten		párense	
_____		_____	
_____		_____	
abran		dibujen	
_____		_____	
_____		_____	

sing	sit down	close	glue	open
stop	cut	paint	stand up	draw

See It, Say It

On your turn roll the die, move your marker, and give the command in Spanish.

- If you can't remember a Spanish word, ask for help and skip a turn.

- The winner is the first player to reach the finish.

- For two to four players.

Action Words

In each box, copy the Spanish action verbs. Then, write the English word below it.

comer	
_____	
_____	

hablar	
_____	
_____	

beber	
_____	
_____	

limpiar	
_____	
_____	

dormir	
_____	
_____	

mirar	
_____	
_____	

tocar	
_____	
_____	

dar	
_____	
_____	

| to touch | to look at | to eat | to give |
| to drink | to speak | to clean | to sleep |

First Sentences

Create original sentences in Spanish using these sentence starters and the verbs in the word bank. You may use one sentence starter more than once. Write the English meanings on the lines below the Spanish.

comer	beber	dormir	tocar
hablar	limpiar	mirar	dar

Sentence Starters

Me gusta _____.	(I like _____.)
No me gusta _____.	(I don't like _____.)
Quiero _____.	(I want _____.)
Necesito _____.	(I need _____.)

1. _____

   _____

2. _____

   _____

3. _____

   _____

4. _____

   _____

5. _____

   _____

Action Words

Refer to the word bank to write the Spanish word that matches each picture.

comer	estudiar	limpiar	mirar	jugar	dar
hablar	beber	dormir	trabajar	tocar	ir

to clean

to touch

to eat

to speak — hablar

to watch

to drink

to give

to sleep

to study

to go

to work

to play

Capitals

Spanish uses capital letters less often than the English language. Follow these rules as your guide.

Capitalization Rules

1. All Spanish sentences begin with capital letters.

2. Names of people begin with capital letters.

3. Names of places (cities, regions, countries, continents) and holidays begin with capital letters.

4. Titles are not capitalized unless abbreviated (*señor–Sr., usted–Ud.*).

5. Some words that are normally capitalized in English may not be capitalized in Spanish (nationalities, religions, languages, months, and days).

Write **sí** if the word should be capitalized. Write **no** if it should remain lowercase.

1. sarah _____

2. inglés _____

3. navidad _____

4. español _____

5. mexicano _____

6. africa _____

7. señor _____

8. enero _____

9. domingo _____

10. católico _____

11. santa fé _____

12. viernes _____

13. méxico _____

14. julio _____

15. colorado _____

16. miguel _____

¿Cómo estás?

bien

así, así

¡Adiós!

mal

Introductions and Greetings

Say the Spanish introductions and greetings out loud.

¡Hola!		**Hello**
¿Cómo te llamas?		**What is your name?**
Me llamo...		**My name is...**
¿Cómo estás?..		**How are you?**

bien   **mal**   **así, así**

¡Adiós!		**Good-bye**

44

Polite Words

Say each Spanish expression out loud.

¿Cuántos años tienes?		**How old are you?**
Tengo seis años.		**I am six years old.**
por favor		**please**
gracias		**thank you**

amigo	**friend**	**amiga**	**friend**
sí **no**		**amigos** 	**friends**
¡Hasta luego!			**See you later!**

45

Introductions Review

Say each expression out loud. Circle the picture that tells the meaning of each word.

gracias		✓	
Tengo seis años.			
por favor			
amigo			
amigos	⊘		
¡Hasta luego!			
amiga			
sí	⊘	✓	

Greetings

Write the English meaning of the Spanish words and phrases.

1. señor _____

2. señora _____

3. señorita _____

4. maestro _____

5. maestra _____

6. ¡Buenos días! _____

7. ¡Buenas tardes! _____

8. ¡Buenas noches! _____

9. Vamos a contar. _____

Mr.	Good night!	Good morning!
Good afternoon!	teacher (female)	teacher (male)
Miss	Let's count.	Mrs.

Draw a picture to show the time of day that you use each expression.

¡Buenos días!	¡Buenas tardes!	¡Buenas noches!

Greetings

Refer to the word bank to translate the Spanish greetings, questions, and answers.

¡Buenos días! _____

¡Buenas tardes! _____

¡Buenas noches! _____

¿Cómo estás? _____

    bien, gracias _____

    mal _____

    así, así _____

¿Cómo te llamas? _____

    Me llamo _____. _____

¿Cuántos años tienes? _____

    Tengo _____ años. _____

adiós _____ hola _____

goodbye	
Good morning!	
I am ____ years old.	
fine, thank you	
Good afternoon!	
hello	
How old are you?	
How are you?	
What is your name?	
My name is ____.	
not well	
ok/so-so	
Good night!	

teacher (m/f)	Miss	no
Mr.	friend (m/f)	please
Mrs.	yes	

Refer to the word bank to translate the Spanish vocabulary.

amigo/amiga _____

sí _____ no _____ por favor _____

señor _____ señora _____

maestro/maestra _____

señorita _____

Days

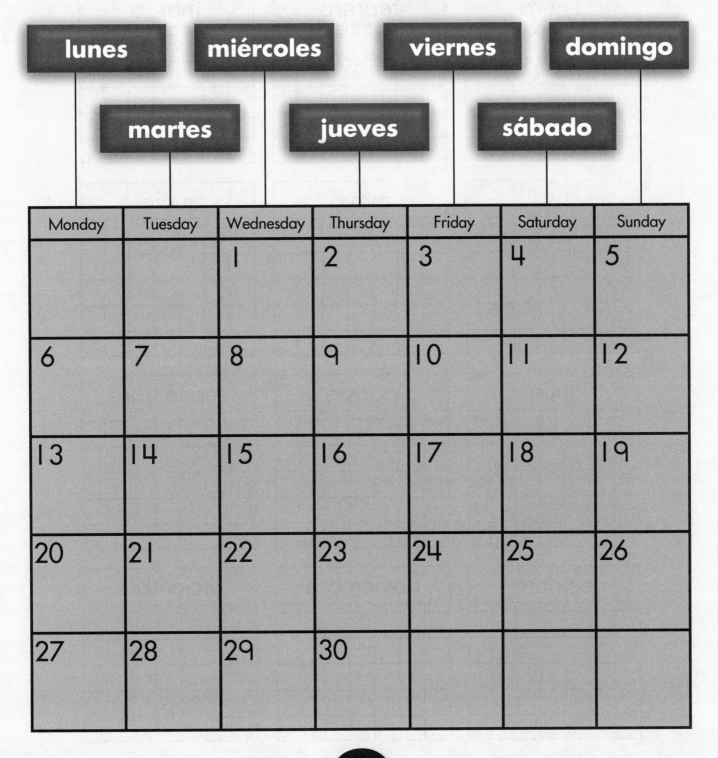

lunes · **martes** · **miércoles** · **jueves** · **viernes** · **sábado** · **domingo**

Monday	Tuesday	Wednesday	Thursday	Friday	Saturday	Sunday
		1	2	3	4	5
6	7	8	9	10	11	12
13	14	15	16	17	18	19
20	21	22	23	24	25	26
27	28	29	30			

Months

enero

febrero

marzo

abril

mayo

junio

julio

agosto

septiembre

octubre

noviembre

diciembre

Calendar Game

On your turn roll the die, move your marker, and say the number and day of the week in Spanish.

- If you can't remember a Spanish word, ask for help and skip a turn.

- The winner is the player who first translates a date from the bottom row.

- For two to four players.

Monday	Tuesday	Wednesday	Thursday	Friday	Saturday	Sunday
	start	1	2	3	4	5
6	7	8	9	10	11	12
13	14	15	16	17	18	19
20	21	22	23	24	25	26
27	28	29	30			

finish line

Yesterday and Today

Write the Spanish words for the days of the week. Remember, in Spanish-speaking countries, Monday is the first day of the week.

miércoles	jueves	domingo	martes
viernes	lunes	sábado	

Monday _____

Tuesday _____

Wednesday _____

Thursday _____

Friday _____

Saturday _____

Sunday _____

If today is Monday, yesterday was Sunday. Complete the following chart by identifying the missing days in Spanish. One is done for you.

ayer (yesterday)	hoy (today)	mañana (tomorrow)
martes	miércoles	jueves
lunes		
		sábado
	domingo	
	jueves	
		martes
viernes		

52

Writing Practice

Copy the following paragraph in your best handwriting. Practice reading it out loud.

Hay doce meses en un año. Diciembre, enero, y febrero son en el invierno. Marzo, abril, y mayo son en la primavera. Junio, julio, y agosto son en el verano. Septiembre, octubre, y noviembre son en el otoño. ¿Cuál es tú favorito mes del año?

Spanish Months

Write the Spanish word for the clue words in the crossword puzzle.

ACROSS
- 4. July
- 9. May
- 10. September
- 11. June
- 12. January

DOWN
- 1. April
- 2. November
- 3. December
- 5. March
- 6. February
- 7. August
- 8. October

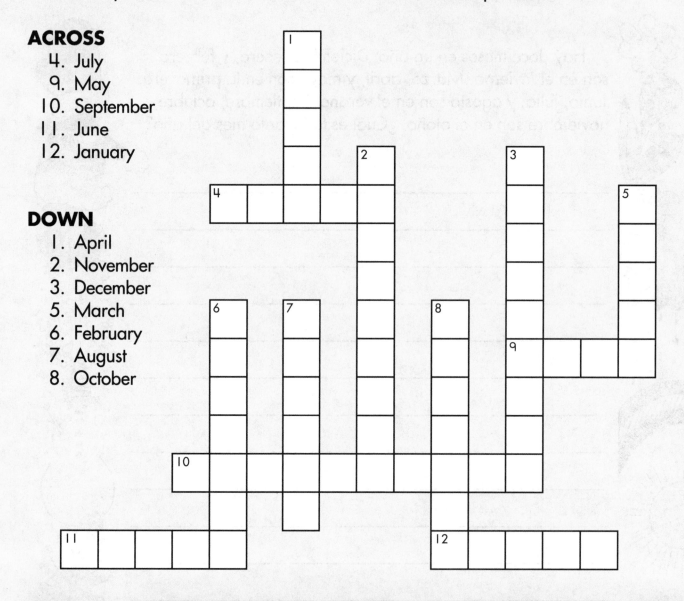

marzo	mayo	diciembre	junio
septiembre	octubre	julio	agosto
abril	enero	febrero	noviembre

negro

blanco

verde

azul

amarillo

café

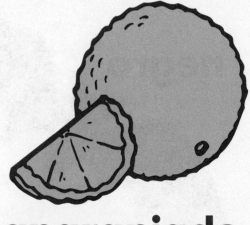

anaranjado

morado

rojo

rosado

Pictures to Color

Color the pictures according to each color word.

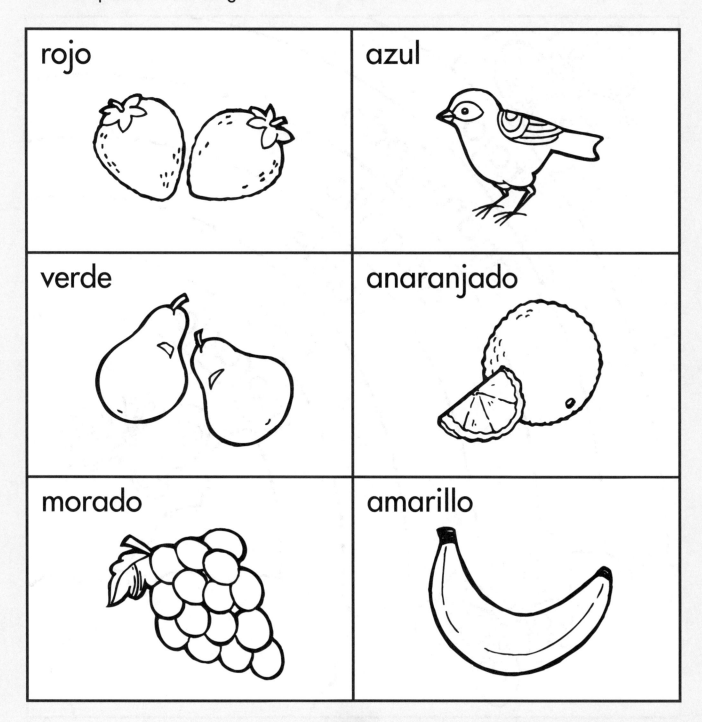

rojo

azul

verde

anaranjado

morado

amarillo

Rainbow Colors

Color the picture according to the color words shown.

rojo
anaranjado
amarillo
verde
azul
morado

Birds of Color

Color the birds according to the words listed.

azul

café

morado

rosado

rojo

verde

negro

amarillo

anaranjado

COLORS

Color Search

Cut out pictures from a magazine that match the colors below. Glue each picture next to the correct color word.

rojo		amarillo	
azul		café	
verde		negro	
anaranjado		blanco	
morado		rosado	

Color Away

Write the English word below the Spanish color listed. Use the words at the bottom to help you. Color the pictures using that color.

rojo means

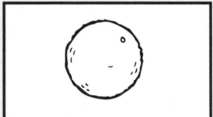

anaranjado means

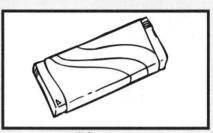

café means

azul means

morado means

blanco means

verde means

amarillo means

rosado means

white	red	orange	green	pink
blue	purple	yellow	brown	black

Color Copy

Copy the following words in the color of each word.

rojo

azul

verde

anaranjado

morado

amarillo

café

negro

blanco

rosado

Color Find

Circle the Spanish color words that you find in the wordsearch. Then, write the English meaning of each word. Words can be across, down, diagonal, and backward.

é	o	a	p	v	o	r	n	u	a	j	v
f	c	x	z	q	d	b	i	a	r	e	a
a	n	n	a	u	i	g	y	i	r	n	n
c	a	c	a	m	l	c	j	d	a	j	y
r	l	o	t	l	a	i	e	r	z	o	r
o	b	g	r	d	b	r	a	t	f	g	l
l	q	d	b	c	o	n	i	s	b	b	f
o	v	s	d	d	j	h	n	l	u	f	o
c	m	y	a	a	o	k	x	e	l	t	j
e	t	r	d	i	o	c	n	k	g	o	o
d	o	o	p	w	q	s	i	d	x	r	r
m	r	o	s	a	d	o	q	k	k	t	o

Spanish Word	English	Spanish Word	English
blanco	_____	amarillo	_____
azul	_____	verde	_____
rojo	_____	café	_____
morado	_____	rosado	_____
anaranjado	_____	negro	_____

Draw and Color

In each box, write the Spanish color word. Use the word bank below to help you. Then, draw and color a picture of something that is usually that color.

red is _____	orange is _____	brown is _____
blue is _____	purple is _____	black is _____
green is _____	yellow is _____	pink is _____

Which Spanish color from the word bank is not used above? _____

blanco	rojo	anaranjado	verde	rosado
azul	morado	amarillo	café	negro

Across the Spectrum

Write the Spanish for each clue word in the crossword puzzle.

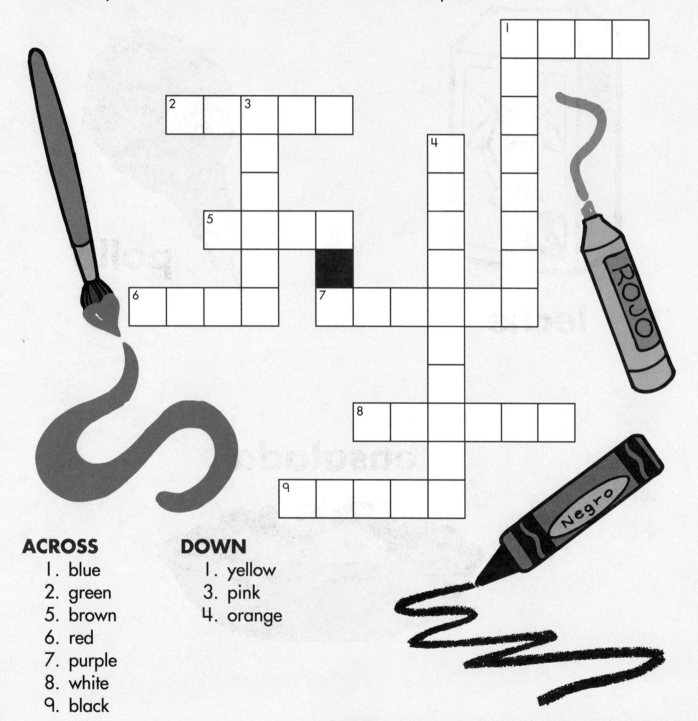

ACROSS
1. blue
2. green
5. brown
6. red
7. purple
8. white
9. black

DOWN
1. yellow
3. pink
4. orange

leche

pollo

ensalada

queso

papa

pan

jugo

Food and Drink

Say the Spanish words for some delicious foods and drinks out loud.

queso		cheese
leche		milk
papa		potato
jugo		juice
pan		bread
pollo		chicken
ensalada		salad

68

Food Meanings

Say each word out loud. Circle the picture that shows the meaning of each word.

papa

ensalada

queso

pan

leche

pollo

jugo

69

Food Words

Say each word out loud. Write the English word next to it.

pollo _____   papa _____   queso _____

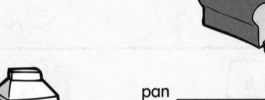

pan _____

leche _____   ensalada _____   jugo _____

Color the blocks with letters.
Do not color the blocks with numbers. What word did you find? _____

7	X	7	7	7	7	7	7	7	7	X	7	7	7	7	7	7	7
7	X	7	7	7	7	7	7	7	7	X	7	7	7	7	7	7	7
7	X	7	7	7	7	7	7	7	7	X	7	7	7	7	7	7	7
7	X	7	X	X	X	7	X	X	X	7	X	7	7	7	X	X	7
7	X	7	X	7	X	7	X	7	7	X	X	X	7	X	7	X	7
7	X	7	X	X	X	7	X	7	7	X	7	X	7	X	X	X	7
7	X	7	X	7	7	7	X	7	7	X	7	X	7	X	7	7	7
7	X	7	X	X	X	7	X	X	X	7	X	7	X	7	X	X	7

FOOD

Food Riddles

Answer the riddles. Use the size and shape of the word blocks along with the answers at the bottom to help you.

I come from an animal.
Kids like to eat my drumstick.
What am I?

I can be full of holes.
Mice like me.
What am I?

I am squeezed from fruit.
Apple is a popular flavor.
What am I?

I come from a cow.
I can be regular or chocolate.
What am I?

You can eat me baked, fried, or mashed.
What am I?

You can eat me plain or with dressing.
What am I?

I rise while baking in an oven.
What am I?

queso   papa   pan   jugo
leche   ensalada   pollo

71

New Food Words

Say each word out loud. Copy each word and color the picture.

sopa

agua

naranja

carne

plátano

manzana

sandwich

A Square Meal

Refer to the word bank to write the name of each food in Spanish.

queso	vegetales
leche	naranja
papa	sopa
pan	agua
jugo	sandwich
pollo	manzana
ensalada	carne
fruta	plátano

Searching for Food

Circle the Spanish words that you find in the wordsearch. Then, write the English meaning of each word. Words can be across, down, diagonal, or backward.

i	v	a	d	a	l	a	s	n	e	p	a
m	a	n	z	a	n	a	s	s	a	g	p
c	a	j	n	a	r	a	n	p	u	o	e
e	o	f	j	v	h	e	a	a	l	a	s
c	h	s	y	i	x	b	b	l	t	e	p
l	a	c	e	w	y	b	o	u	l	t	l
p	e	r	i	u	m	q	r	a	a	v	á
a	t	c	n	w	q	f	t	m	d	a	t
n	u	i	h	e	d	e	o	s	x	p	a
r	m	r	t	e	g	n	i	g	l	o	n
f	r	s	k	e	j	o	a	w	u	s	o
i	r	a	v	p	a	h	h	s	i	j	v

Spanish Word	English	Spanish Word	English
queso	_____	papa	_____
jugo	_____	ensalada	_____
sopa	_____	sandwich	_____
carne	_____	fruta	_____
leche	_____	pan	_____
pollo	_____	naranja	_____
agua	_____	manzana	_____
plátano	_____	vegetales	_____

Eat It Up

Write the Spanish for the clue words in the crossword puzzle.

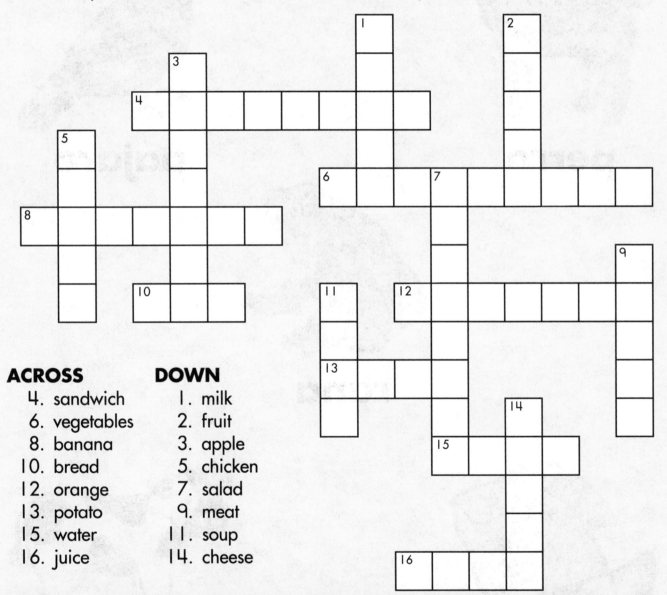

ACROSS
4. sandwich
6. vegetables
8. banana
10. bread
12. orange
13. potato
15. water
16. juice

DOWN
1. milk
2. fruit
3. apple
5. chicken
7. salad
9. meat
11. soup
14. cheese

ensalada	sandwich	sopa	fruta	papa	pollo
pan	plátano	leche	jugo	queso	
carne	naranja	manzana	agua	vegetales	

perro

pájaro

rana

pez

vaca

abeja

pato

gato

oso

caballo

Animal Art

Choose four animals and draw each animal in its home. Label it with the Spanish animal word.

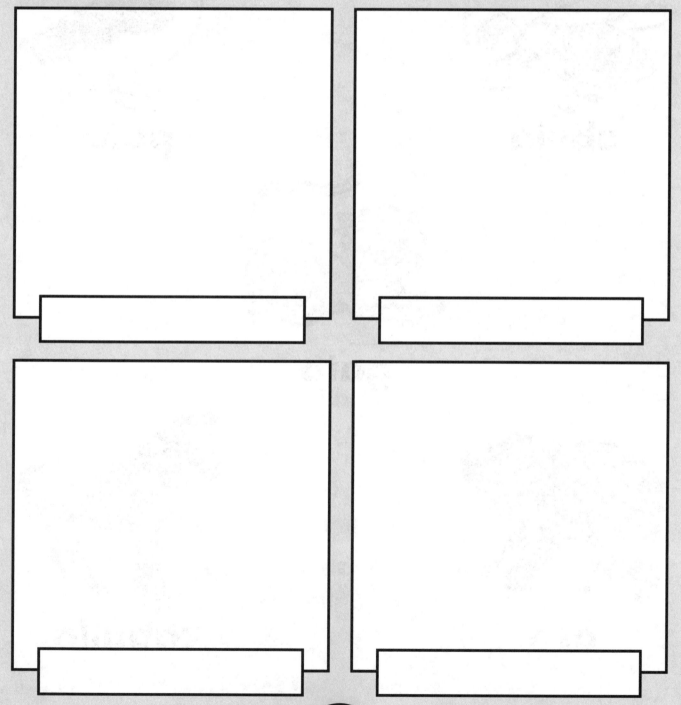

Animal Crossword

Use the picture clues to complete the puzzle. Choose from the Spanish words at the bottom of the page.

| gato | perro | pájaro |
| pez | pato | culebra |

Use the Clues

Answer the questions. Use the clues and the Spanish words at the bottom of the page. You may use answers more than once.

1. Both words begin with the same letter, and both animals have feathers.

_____   _____

2. These two animals walk and are house pets.

_____   _____

3. Both animals begin with the same letter. One quacks and the other barks.

_____   _____

4. Both of these animals like to live in the water.

_____   _____

5. These animals do not have fur or feathers.

_____   _____

6. The first animal likes to chase and catch the second animal. They both end with the letter **o**.

_____   _____

gato	perro	pájaro
pez	pato	culebra

Pet Parade

In each box, copy the name of each animal in Spanish. Write the Spanish words next to the English words at the bottom of the page.

pájaro	bird	caballo	horse
perro	dog	oso	bear
rana	frog	gato	cat
vaca	cow	pato	duck
abeja	bee	pez	fish

Write the Spanish words from above next to the English words.

cat _____   cow _____   frog _____

dog _____   horse _____   bee _____

bird _____   bear _____

fish _____   duck _____

81

Three Little Kittens

Draw a picture to match the Spanish phrase in each box.

seis pájaros	cuatro perros
nueve abejas	siete osos
tres gatos	dos vacas
cinco patos	ocho caballos
diez ranas	un pez

Rainbow Roundup

Copy the following Spanish sentences on the lines provided. Then, write the English meanings. Use a Spanish-English dictionary if you need help.

I. El oso es blanco. _____

_____

2. El puerco es rosado. _____

_____

3. La rana es roja. _____

_____

4. La tortuga es verde. _____

_____

5. El dinosaurio es azul. _____

_____

6. El gato es anaranjado. _____

_____

7. La gallina es amarilla. _____

_____

8. El caballo es café. _____

_____

9. La mariposa es morada. _____

_____

vestido

gorro

camisa

calcetines

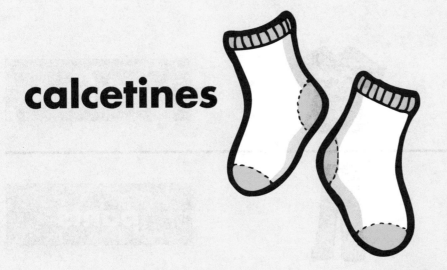

zapatos

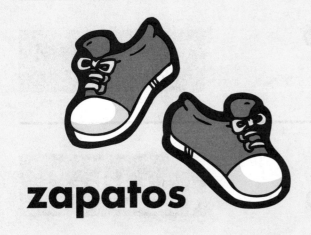

pantalones

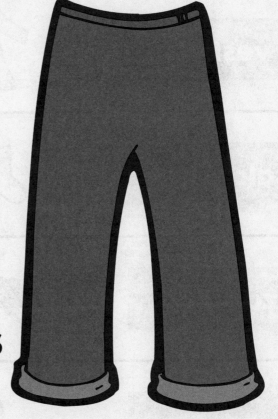

Clothing

Say each word out loud.

camisa		shirt
pantalones		pants
vestido		dress
calcetines		socks
zapatos		shoes
gorro		cap

Clothes to Color

Cut out pictures and glue them next to the correct words.

camisa

zapatos

calcetines

vestido

pantalones

gorro

Color the blocks with letters.
Do not color the blocks with numbers. What word did you find? _____

8	8	8	8	8	8	8	8	8	8	8	8	8	8	8	8	8	8	8	8	8	8	8	8
8	8	X	X	X	8	X	X	X	8	X	X	X	8	X	X	X	8	X	X	X	8		
8	8	X	8	X	8	X	8	X	8	X	8	X	8	X	8	X	8	X	8	X	8		
8	8	X	X	X	8	X	8	X	8	8	8	X	8	8	8	X	8	X	8				
8	8	8	8	X	8	X	X	X	8	X	8	8	8	X	X	X	8						
8	8	X	8	X	8	8	8	8	8	8	8	8	8	8	8	8	8						
8	8	X	X	X	8	8	8	8	8	8	8	8	8	8	8	8	8						

Clothing

Say each word out loud. Copy each word and color the picture.

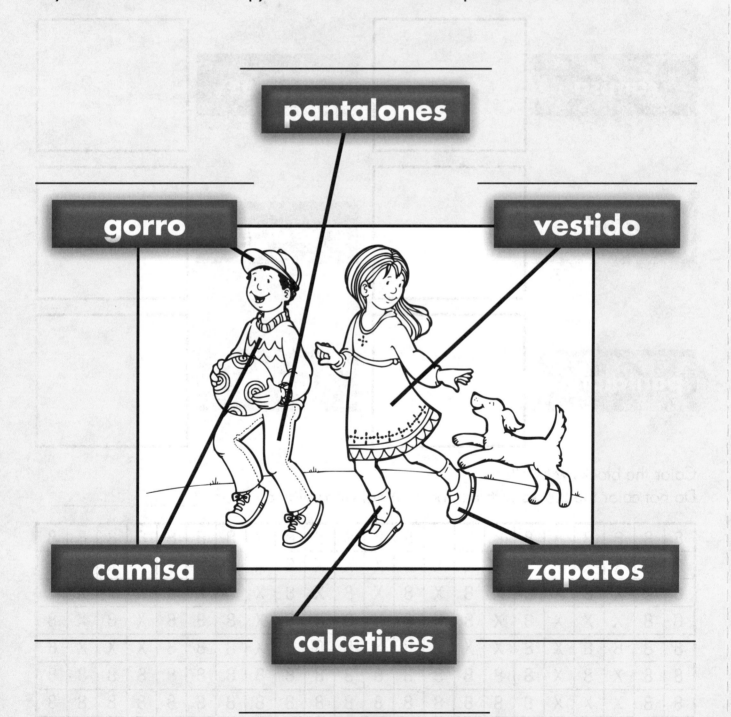

pantalones

gorro

vestido

camisa

zapatos

calcetines

Clothing

Say each word out loud. Copy each word and color the picture.

abrigo

chaqueta

falda

guantes

botas

pantalones
cortos

Remember These?

Fill in the blanks with the missing letters. Use the Spanish clothing words at the bottom to help you. One is done for you.

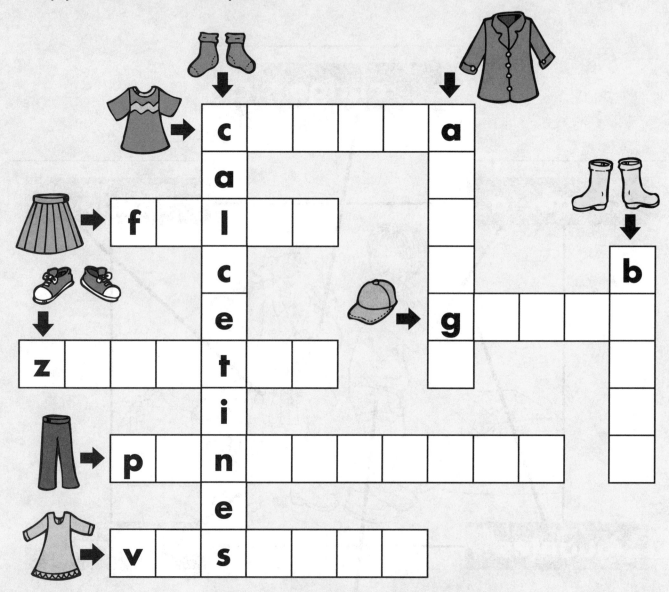

| camisa | vestido | pantalones | falda |
| zapatos | gorro | abrigo | botas |

Clothes Closet

Refer to the word bank and write the Spanish word for each item of clothing pictured.

vestido	**calcetines**	**botas**	**zapatos**
sombrero	**cinturón**	**falda**	**chaqueta**
guantes	**pantalones cortos**	**pantalones**	**camisa**

shirt		pants	
shorts		hat	
socks		skirt	
shoes		belt	
boots		dress	
gloves		jacket	

Colorful Clothing

Copy each sentence in Spanish on the first line. Write the English meaning on the second line. Use a Spanish-English dictionary if you need help.

1. El vestido es rojo. _____

_____

2. La camisa es café. _____

_____

3. El sombrero es morado. _____

_____

4. La falda es verde. _____

_____

5. El vestido es rosado. _____

_____

6. La chaqueta es azul. _____

_____

7. Los calcetines son amarillos. _____

_____

8. El cinturón es anaranjado. _____

_____

9. Las botas son blancas. _____

_____

Clothes Closet

Circle the Spanish words that you find in the puzzle. Write the English meanings at the bottom of the page next to the Spanish words from the puzzle.

v	s	q	o	d	i	t	s	e	v	f	a	o
i	e	a	c	o	y	f	f	n	a	s	g	g
r	n	b	t	j	n	c	l	l	e	i	j	u
x	ó	x	s	o	r	a	d	n	r	q	r	a
s	r	h	u	e	b	a	i	b	l	y	i	n
a	u	t	g	c	n	t	a	l	p	g	b	t
i	t	c	y	g	e	o	a	g	n	z	o	e
l	n	o	m	c	b	o	l	s	o	m	s	s
a	i	v	l	l	k	o	v	a	i	r	x	v
d	c	a	u	e	m	l	n	s	t	m	r	a
n	c	s	z	a	p	a	t	o	s	n	a	o
a	a	k	a	t	e	u	q	a	h	c	a	c
s	g	u	f	a	t	e	z	i	m	a	c	p

Spanish Word	English	Spanish Word	English
abrigo	_____	sandalias	_____
guantes	_____	calcetines	_____
blusa	_____	falda	_____
chaqueta	_____	vestido	_____
pantalones	_____	camisa	_____
botas	_____	gorro	_____
cinturón	_____	zapatos	_____

ojos

nariz

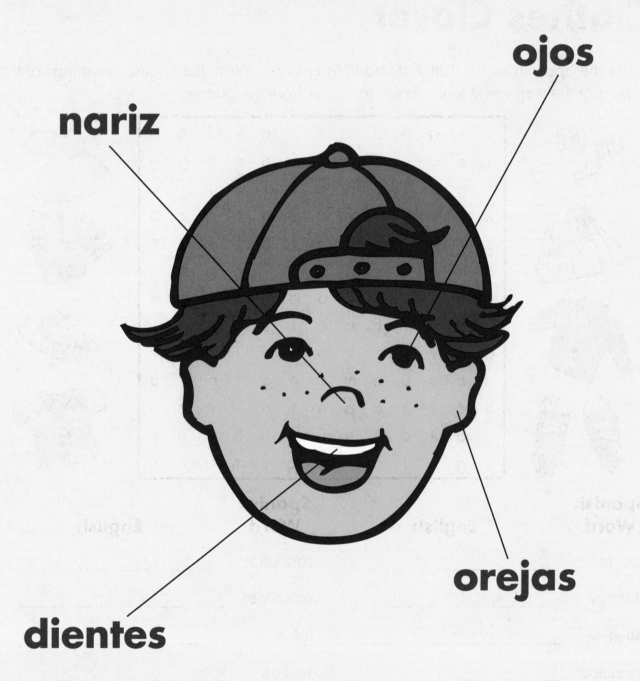

orejas

dientes

cara

boca

pelo

What's on Your Face?

Say each word out loud. Copy each word.

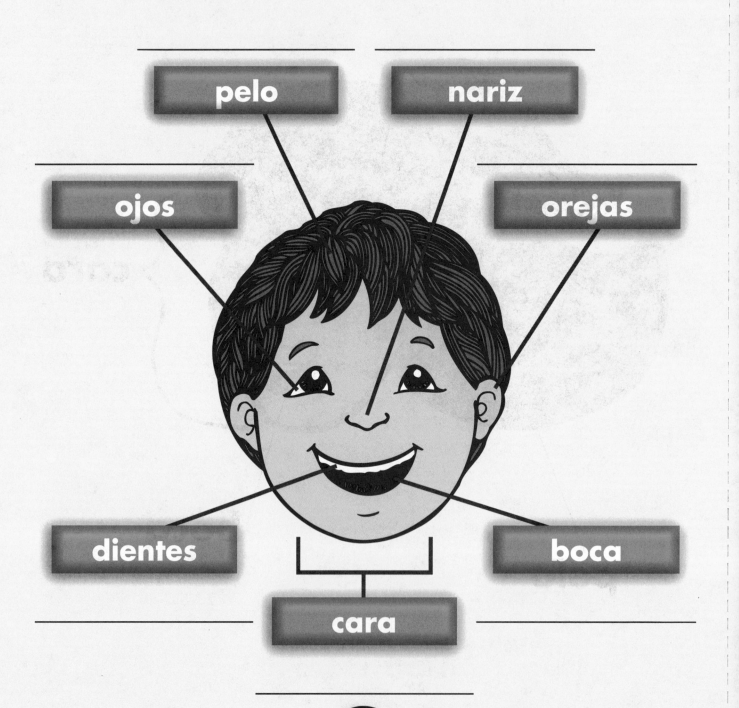

Face Riddles

Can you guess the answers to the following riddles? Use the size and shape of the letter blocks to write the Spanish word. The answers at the bottom will help you.

There are two of me.
Sometimes, I need glasses.
What am I?

I like to be washed and combed.
What am I?

I help hold up glasses.
When I feel an itch, I sneeze.
What am I?

Everyone's looks a little different, in spite of the shape. What am I?

We grow, get loose, fall out, and grow again.
What are we?

"Open wide" is often said when I am too small.
What am I?

Does your mom always tell you to wash behind us?
What are we?

nariz	pelo	dientes	boca
ojos	orejas	cara	

97

A Blank Face

Fill in the blanks with the missing letters. Use the Spanish words below to help you.

| nariz | pelo | dientes | ojos | orejas | cara | boca |

Which word didn't you use? _____

Color each block that has a letter **k** inside. Do not color the blocks with numbers.

What hidden word did you find? _____

k	5	5	5	5	5	5	5	5	5	5	5	5	5	5	5
k	5	5	5	5	5	5	5	5	5	5	5	5	5	5	5
k	5	5	5	5	5	5	5	5	5	5	5	5	5	5	5
k	k	k	5	k	k	k	5	k	k	k	5	k	k	k	5
k	5	k	5	k	5	k	5	k	5	5	5	k	5	k	5
k	5	k	5	k	5	k	5	k	5	5	5	k	5	k	5
k	k	k	5	k	k	k	5	k	k	k	5	k	k	k	k

Head to Toe

Using the word banks, label the parts of the face and body. Use the glossary to help you.

cara	boca	dientes	pelo
ojos	nariz	orejas	

cuerpo	cabeza	mano	pierna	hombro
brazo	dedo	pie	rodilla	estómago

BODY

Knees and Toes

Write the Spanish words for the clues in the crossword puzzle.

cuerpo	cabeza	mano	pierna	hombro
brazo	dedo	pie	rodilla	estómago

ACROSS
2. foot
3. body
5. knee
6. head
7. shoulder
9. hand

DOWN
1. finger or toe
2. leg
4. stomach
8. arm

100

How Are You?

Label each facial feature with a Spanish word from the word bank.

_____ _____ _____ _____

cara	pelo
ojos	dientes
boca	orejas
nariz	

_____ _____ _____

Copy the Spanish word that matches each face pictured.

happy
alegre

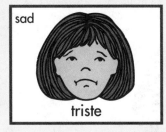
sad
triste

crying
llorando

_____ _____ _____

smiling
sonriendo

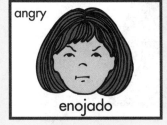
angry
enojado

thinking
pensando

_____ _____ _____

101

padre

madre

hermano

hermana

abuelo

abuela

Family Words

Say each family word out loud.

| madre | | mother |

| padre | | father |

| hermana | | sister |

| hermano | | brother |

| abuela | | grandmother |

| abuelo | | grandfather |

Matching Family

Cut out a picture of a family from a magazine. Glue each picture next to the correct word.

padre

hermana

madre

abuelo

hermano

abuelo

Color the blocks with letters.
Do not color the blocks with numbers. What word did you find? _____

2	2	2	2	2	2	2	2	2	2	2	2	m	2	2	2	2	2	2	2	2
2	2	2	2	2	2	2	2	2	2	2	2	m	2	2	2	2	2	2	2	2
m	m	m	m	m	2	m	m	m	2	2	m	m	m	2	m	m	m	2	m	m
m	2	m	2	m	2	m	2	m	2	2	m	2	m	2	m	2	m	2	m	2	m
m	2	m	2	m	2	m	2	m	2	2	m	2	m	2	m	2	2	2	m	m	m
m	2	m	2	m	2	m	2	m	2	2	m	2	m	2	m	2	2	2	m	2	2
m	2	m	2	m	2	m	m	m	m	2	m	m	m	2	m	2	2	2	m	m	m

Family

Copy each word and color the pictures.

madre

padre

_____

_____

abuelo

abuela

_____

_____

hermana

hermano

_____

_____

Let's learn two new words.

chico

chica

106

Listen Well

Say each word out loud. Circle the picture for each Spanish word.

padre

abuelo

hermana

chica

abuela

madre

hermano

chico

My Family

Write the Spanish word for each clue in the crossword puzzle.

ACROSS
- 2. son
- 3. aunt
- 5. sister
- 7. grandmother
- 8. brother
- 10. cousins

DOWN
- 1. mother
- 2. daughter
- 4. family
- 6. grandfather
- 9. uncle
- 10. father

familia	hermano	hijo	tía
primos	madre	tío	abuelo
padre	hermana	hija	abuela

FAMILY

Family Tree

Refer to the word bank to write the Spanish word that matches each picture.

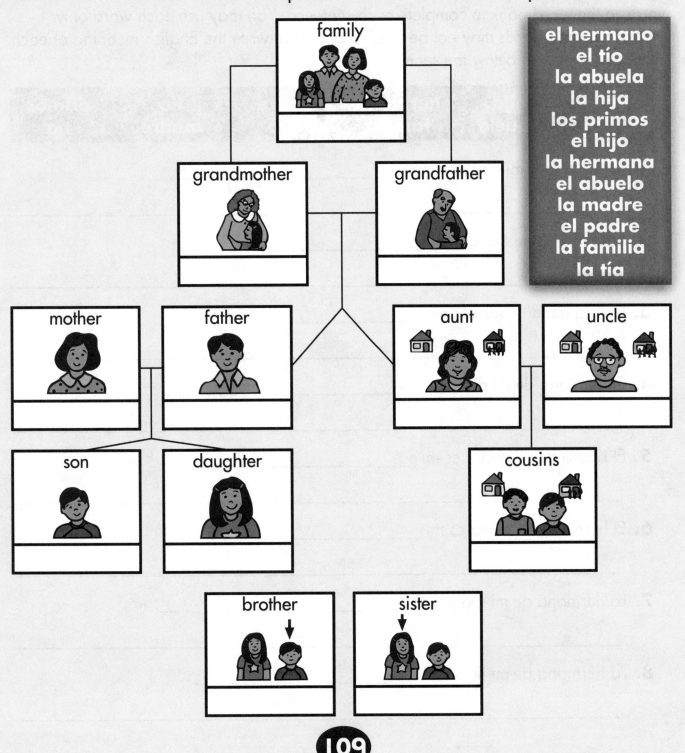

el hermano
el tío
la abuela
la hija
los primos
el hijo
la hermana
el abuelo
la madre
el padre
la familia
la tía

Relationships

How are the following people related? Read the Spanish sentences carefully. Use the words in the word bank to complete each sentence. You may use each word only once, and some words may not be used at all. Then, write the English meaning of each sentence on the line below the sentence.

hermano	hija	hermana	padre	tío	primos
abuela	abuelo	familia	hijo	madre	tía

1. La madre de mi madre es mi _____.

_____

2. Los hijos de mi tío son mis _____.

_____

3. La hija de mi madre es mi _____.

_____

4. El hermano de mi padre es mi _____.

_____

5. El padre de mi padre es mi _____.

_____

6. El hermano de mi tío es mi _____.

_____

7. La hermana de mi madre es mi _____.

_____

8. La hermana de mi tía es mi _____.

_____

biblioteca

escuela

parque

tienda

casa

museo

Picture This

Say each word out loud. Circle the picture that shows the meaning of each word.

museo

escuela

tienda

parque

biblioteca

casa

Places, Please

Cut out pictures that match the words below. Glue each picture next to the correct word.

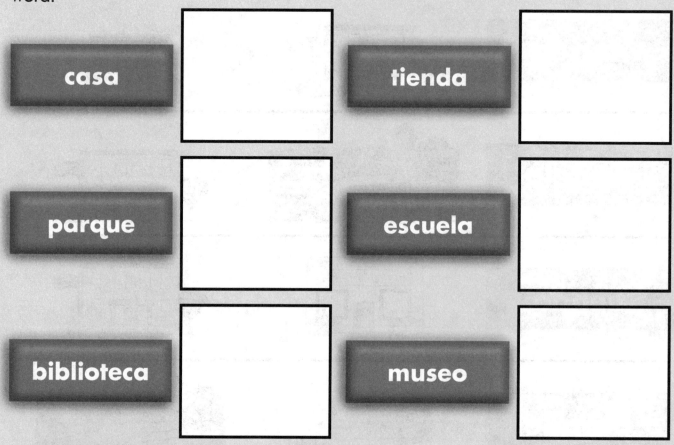

casa

tienda

parque

escuela

biblioteca

museo

Color the blocks with letters.
Do not color the blocks with numbers. What word did you find? _____

9	9	9	9	9	9	9	9	9	9	9	9	9	9	9	9	9	9
Y	Y	Y	9	Y	Y	Y	9	9	Y	Y	Y	9	Y	Y	Y	Y	9
Y	9	Y	9	Y	9	Y	9	9	Y	9	9	9	Y	9	Y	Y	9
Y	9	9	9	Y	9	Y	9	9	Y	Y	Y	9	Y	9	Y	Y	9
Y	9	Y	9	Y	9	Y	9	9	9	9	Y	9	Y	9	Y	Y	9
Y	Y	Y	9	Y	Y	Y	9	Y	Y	Y	Y	9	Y	Y	Y	Y	Y
9	9	9	9	9	9	9	9	9	9	9	9	9	9	9	9	9	9

Places to Go

Say each word out loud. Copy each word and color the picture.

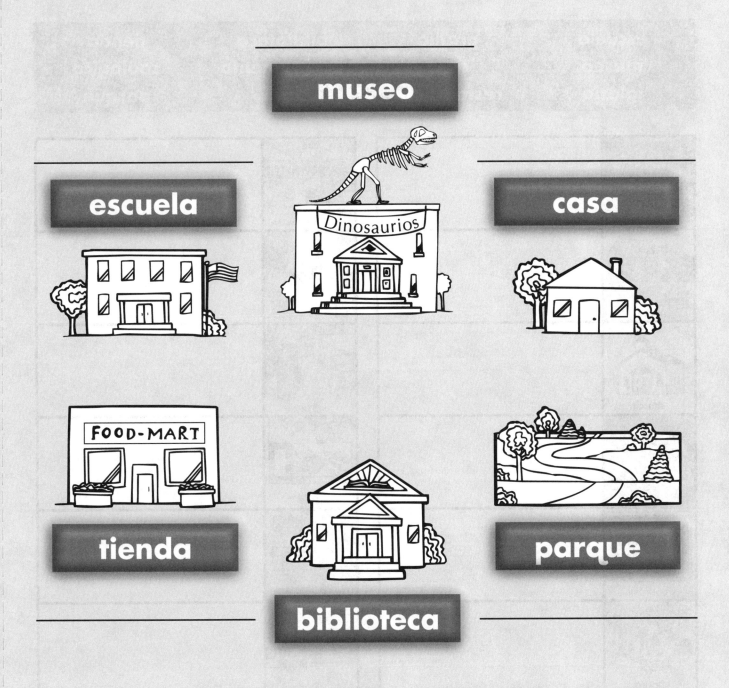

museo

escuela

casa

tienda

biblioteca

parque

Where Am I?

Refer to the word bank and write the Spanish word for each place in the community pictured.

escuela	granja	biblioteca	tienda
museo	casa	apartamento	zoológico
iglesia	restaurante	cine	parque

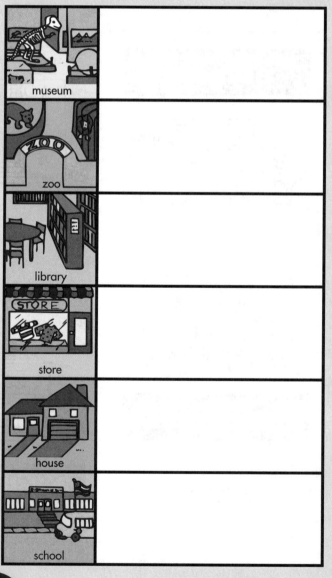

Around the House

Copy the Spanish words. Then, write the English words below them.

casa

_____

_____

cocina

_____

_____

sala

_____

_____

dormitorio

_____

_____

sofá

_____

_____

cama

_____

_____

lámpara

_____

_____

cuchara

_____

_____

| couch | kitchen | lamp | spoon |
| bedroom | bed | house | living room |

117

Around the Block

Write the Spanish words from the word bank that fit in these word blocks. Write the English below the blocks.

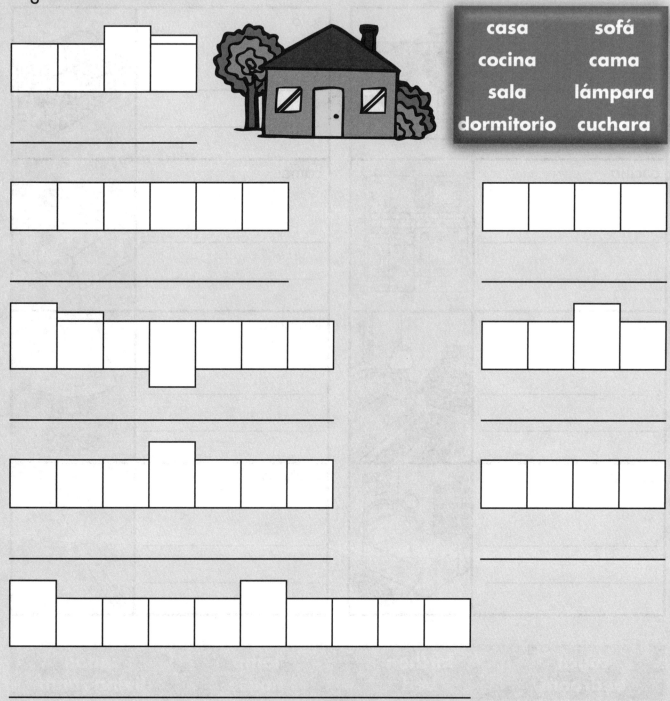

casa	sofá
cocina	cama
sala	lámpara
dormitorio	cuchara

A Blue House

Copy the sentences in Spanish on the first lines. Write the sentences in English on the second lines.

1. La casa es azul. _____

_____

2. La sala es café. _____

_____

3. El dormitorio es morado. _____

_____

4. La cuchara es verde. _____

_____

5. El sofá es rosado. _____

_____

6. La cama es azul. _____

_____

7. La lámpara es amarilla. _____

_____

Challenge:

La fruta está en la cocina. _____

_____

_____

Home, Sweet Home

At the bottom of each picture, copy the Spanish word.

 dormitorio

 vaso

 cocina

 casa

_____ _____ _____ _____

 sala

 baño

 toalla

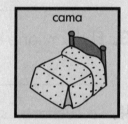 cama

_____ _____ _____ _____

 estufa

 televisión

 lámpara

 teléfono

_____ _____ _____ _____

Write the Spanish word after each room or household item.

bathroom _____

towel _____

television _____

bedroom _____

living room _____

kitchen _____

lamp _____

bed _____

telephone _____

stove _____

glass _____

house _____

120

libro

lápiz

tijeras

borrador

mesa

silla

Classroom Things

Say each word out loud.

| silla |  | chair |

| libro |  | book |

| mesa |  | table |

| lápiz | | pencil |

| tijeras |  | scissors |

| borrador | | eraser |

123

Draw and Color Your Classroom

Draw and color a picture for each word listed. Which ones do you have in your classroom? Circle them.

silla

libro

mesa

lápiz

tijeras

borrador

Classroom Things

Copy each word and color the picture.

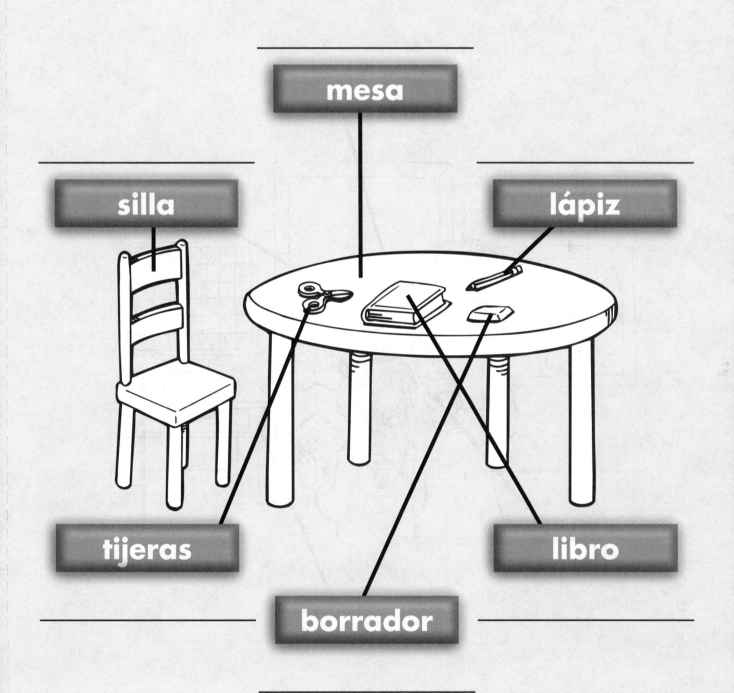

New Classroom Words

Say each word out loud. Copy each word and color the picture.

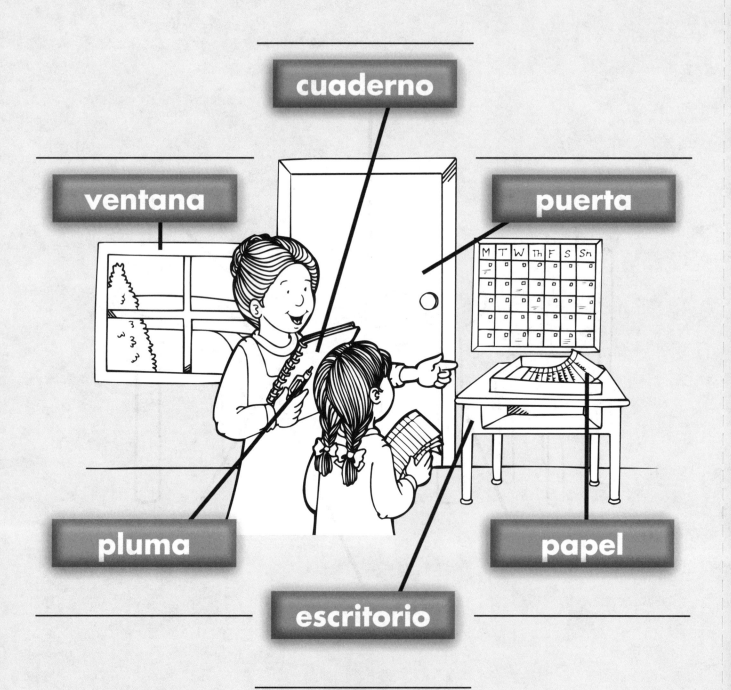

cuaderno

ventana

puerta

pluma

papel

escritorio

Listen Carefully

Say each word out loud. Circle the picture that tells the meaning of each word.

libro			
tijeras			
ventana			
silla			
pluma			
lápiz			
cuaderno			
mesa			
puerta			

Show and Tell

Write the Spanish for each clue in the crossword puzzle.

ACROSS

1. notebook
5. scissors
7. pen
8. eraser
10. pencil
11. table
12. chair

DOWN

2. desk
3. window
4. book
6. door
9. paper

escritorio   mesa   libro   silla   tijeras   puerta

lápiz   ventana   borrador   cuaderno   papel   pluma

Pencil and Paper

Copy the following sentences in Spanish. Then, write the English meanings.

1. El libro es rojo. _____

_____

2. La silla es café. _____

_____

3. El cuaderno es morado. _____

_____

4. La mesa es verde. _____

_____

5. El lápiz es rosado. _____

_____

6. El borrador es amarillo. _____

_____

7. La ventana es azul. _____

_____

8. El escritorio es anaranjado. _____

_____

9. El papel es blanco. _____

_____

129

Around the Room

In each box, copy the Spanish word for the classroom object pictured.

silla		mesa	
puerta		pluma	
ventana		borrador	
lápiz		cuaderno	
papel		libro	
escritorio		tijeras	

Write the Spanish words from above next to the English words.

window _____ chair _____ table _____

eraser _____ scissors _____ door _____

desk _____ pen _____ notebook _____

paper _____ book _____ pencil _____

130

A Fitting Design

Write the Spanish words from the word bank that fit in these word blocks. Write the English meanings below the blocks.

ventana	silla	pluma	mesa	cuaderno
papel	tijeras	libro	puerta	lápiz

Where's My Pencil?

Circle the Spanish words that you find in the word search. Then, write the English meaning of each word. Words can be across, down, diagonal, or backward.

```
w  p  p  a  r  t  m  a  m  u  l  p
r  u  x  f  s  o  t  r  h  h  o  n
x  e  d  e  j  e  d  j  j  i  m  l
o  r  a  h  v  z  m  a  r  a  o  u
o  t  o  f  e  i  f  o  r  m  i  l
n  a  r  t  s  e  t  s  l  r  y  o
r  p  b  f  p  i  a  m  l  h  o  v
e  i  i  g  r  r  e  p  n  d  m  b
d  w  l  c  e  y  e  a  l  l  i  s
a  q  s  j  l  e  f  l  e  p  a  p
u  e  i  l  a  p  i  z  i  m  t  d
c  t  v  e  n  t  a  n  a  i  n  i
```

Spanish Word	English	Spanish Word	English
ventana	_____	pluma	_____
borrador	_____	libro	_____
escritorio	_____	mesa	_____
papel	_____	puerta	_____
silla	_____	cuaderno	_____
tijeras	_____	lápiz	_____

Classroom Clutter

Draw a picture to illustrate each of the Spanish words. Refer to the word bank at the bottom of the page to help you.

silla	ventana
mesa	puerta
tijeras	papel
libro	cuaderno
lápiz	escritorio
borrador	pluma

eraser	door	scissors	pen	window	paper
chair	notebook	pencil	desk	book	table

Songs and Chants

Diez (veinte) amigos
(to the tune of "Ten Little Fingers")

Uno, dos, tres amigos,
cuatro, cinco, seis amigos,
siete, ocho, nueve amigos,
diez amigos son.

Diez, nueve, ocho amigos,
siete, seis, cinco amigos,
cuatro, tres, dos amigos,
un amigo es.

Once, doce, trece amigos,
catorce, quince, dieciséis amigos,
diecisiete, dieciocho,
diecinueve amigos,
veinte amigos son.

Community Song
(to the tune of "Here We Go 'Round the Mulberry Bush")

Escuela is school,
museo — museum,
casa is house,
tienda is store,
biblioteca is library,
parque is the park for me!

Songs and Chants

Family Song
(to the tune of "Are You Sleeping?")

Padre — father,
madre — mother,
chico — boy,
chica — girl,
abuelo is grandpa,
abuela is grandma.
Our family, our family.

Hermano — brother,
hermana — sister,
chico — boy,
chica — girl,
padre y madre,
abuelo y abuela.
Our family, our family.

Los días de la semana
(to the tune of "Clementine")

Domingo, lunes,
martes, miércoles,
jueves, viernes, sábado,
domingo, lunes,
martes, miércoles,
jueves, viernes, sábado. (*Repitan*)

Songs and Chants

¡Hola! Means Hello
(to the tune of "London Bridge")

¡Hola! means hello-o-o, hello-o-o, hello-o-o.
¡Hola! means hello-o-o. *¡Hola, amigos!*

¡Adiós! Means Good-bye
(to the tune of "London Bridge")

¡Adiós! means goo-ood-bye, goo-ood-bye, goo-ood-bye.
¡Adiós! means goo-ood-bye. *¡Adiós, amigos!*

¡Adiós!

Songs and Chants

Animals Song
(to the tune of "This Old Man")

Gato — cat,
perro — dog,
pájaro is a flying bird,
pez is a fish, and
pato is a duck,
culebra is a slinky snake.

Colors Song
(to the tune of "Twinke, Twinkle Little Star")

Red is *rojo*,	green is *verde*,
purple, *morado*,	brown, *café*;
yellow, *amarillo*,	blue, *azul*,
pink is *rosado*,	orange, *anaranjado*;
white is *blanco*,	black is *negro*,
colors, *colores*,	colors, *colores*.

Songs and Chants

Classroom Objects Song
(to the tune of "The Farmer in the Dell")

A *silla* is a chair;
A *libro* is a book;
A *mesa* is a table in our classroom.

A *lápiz* is a pencil;
Tijeras is a scissors;
A *borrador* is an eraser in our classroom.

Clothing Song
(to the tune of "Skip to My Lou")

Camisa — shirt,   *pantalones* — pants,
vestido — dress,   *calcetines* — socks,
zapatos — shoes,   *gorro* — cap
These are the clothes that we wear.

Songs and Chants

Food Song

(to the tune of "She'll Be Coming 'Round the Mountain")

Queso is cheese, yum, yum, yum. (clap, clap)
Leche is milk, yum, yum, yum. (clap, clap)
Papa is potato.
Jugo is juice.
Pan is bread, yum, yum, yum! (clap, clap)

Pollo is chicken, yum, yum, yum. (clap, clap)
Ensalada is salad, yum, yum, yum. (clap, clap)
Queso, leche, papa,
jugo, pan, pollo, ensalada,
yum, yum, yum, yum, yum! (clap, clap)

Face Song

(to the tune of "Here We Go
'Round the Mulberry Bush")

Ojos — eyes, *boca* — mouth,
nariz — nose, *dientes* — teeth,
orejas — ears, *pelo* — hair,
cara is my face.

Songs and Chants

¡Hola, chicos!
(to the tune of "Goodnight Ladies")

¡Hola, chico! ¡Hola, chica!
¡Hola, chicos! ¿Cómo están hoy?
¡Hola, chico! ¡Hola, chica!
¡Hola, chicos! ¿Cómo están hoy?

Alphabet Song
(to the tune of "B-I-N-G-O")

A	B	C	D	E	F	G
(There	was	a	farmer	had	a	dog)

H		I	J		K	
(and Bin-		go	was his		name-o.)	

L	M	N	Ñ	O		
(B	I	N	G	O)		

P	Q	R	S	T		
(B	I	N	G	O)		

U	V	W				
(B	I	N G O)				

X	Y		Z			
(and	Bingo was his		name-o.)			

Songs and Chants

Cumpleaños feliz
(to the tune of "Happy Birthday")

Cumpleaños feliz,
Cumpleaños feliz,
Te deseamos todos,
Cumpleaños feliz.

Así me lavo las manos
(to the tune of "Here We Go Round the Mulberry Bush")

Así me lavo las manos, las manos, las manos   (Use hand motions to show hand washing)
Así me lavo las manos, por la mañana.
Así me lavo la cara, la cara, la cara   (Use hand motions to show face washing)
Así me lavo la cara, por la mañana.
Así me lavo los pies, los pies, los pies   (Use different body parts that students pick)
(los brazos, el estómago, etc.)

Songs

Fray Felipe
(to the tune of "Are You Sleeping?")

Fray Felipe, Fray Felipe, ¿Duermes tú, duermes tú?
Toca la campana, toca la campana, tan, tan, tan, tan, tan, tan.

Fray Francisco, Fray Francisco, ¿Duermes tú, duermes tú?
Toca la campana, toca la campana, tan, tan, tan, tan, tan, tan.

Chants

Body Chant

Cabeza, hombros, rodillas, dedos, rodillas, dedos, rodillas, dedos
Cabeza, hombros, rodillas, dedos
Ojos, orejas, boca, nariz.

Number Chant

Dos y dos son cuatro, cuatro y dos son seis, seis y dos son ocho, y ocho más, dieciséis.
(Two and two are four, four and two are six, six and two are eight, and eight more, sixteen.)

Clothing Chant

Abrigo rosado, vestido blanco,
camisa café, sombrero morado,
blusas verdes, pantalones rojos,
botas azules, zapatos negros.

Pink coat, white dress,
brown shirt, purple hat,
green blouses, red pants,
blue boots, black shoes.

Adjective Chant

La casa es grande, la mesa—pequeña,
la puerta—cerrada, la ventana abierta.

The house is big, the table—small,
the door—closed, the window—open.

Papa Chant

Yo como una papa, no como a mi papá.
    I eat a potato, I don't eat my dad.
Una papa es comida, un papá es un padre.
    A papa is a potato, a papá is a father.

*Due to differences in languages, literal translations of chants may lose meaning and/or the sense of rhythm.

143

Learning Cards

In this section, students will be able to review the topics they have learned earlier in this book. Beginning on page 145, students will be able to cut out and create illustrated books with the vocabulary words from *Exploring Spanish*.

Beginning on page 191, students can cut out flashcards with a Spanish word on one side and the definition in English on the other side. These flash cards are ideal for both individual and group practice.

Table of Contents

Introductions and Greetings

¡Hola!

¿Cómo te llamas?

Me llamo

¡Adiós!

¿Cómo estás?

bien

Introductions and Greetings

mal

así, así

¿Cuántos años tienes?

Tengo _____ años.

sí

no

Introductions and Greetings

por favor

gracias

amigo

amiga

amigos

¡Hasta luego!

Numbers

0 cero	**1 uno**
2 dos	**3 tres**
4 cuatro 	**5 cinco** 

Numbers and The Face (cara)

6 seis

7 siete

8 ocho

9 nueve

10 diez

cara

Numbers

11 once

12 doce

13 trece

14 catorce

15 quince

16 dieciséis

Numbers and Family

17 diecisiete

18 dieciocho

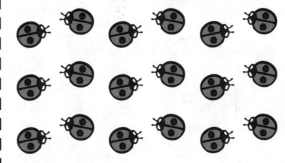

19 diecinueve

20 veinte

hermano

hermana

Family

padre

madre

hermano

hermana

abuelo

abuela

Incredible!

Incredible!

Incredible!

Incredible!

The Face

ojos

boca

nariz

dientes

orejas

pelo

Colors

rojo

azul

verde

anaranjado

morado

amarillo

Colors and Food

café

negro

blanco

rosado

pollo

queso

Food

ensalada

pan

jugo

leche

papa

naranja

Food

carne

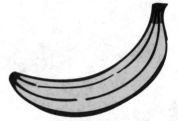

plátano

sopa

agua

sandwich

manzana

Classroom Objects

silla

mesa

tijeras

libro

lápiz

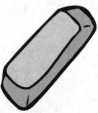

borrador

Classroom Objects

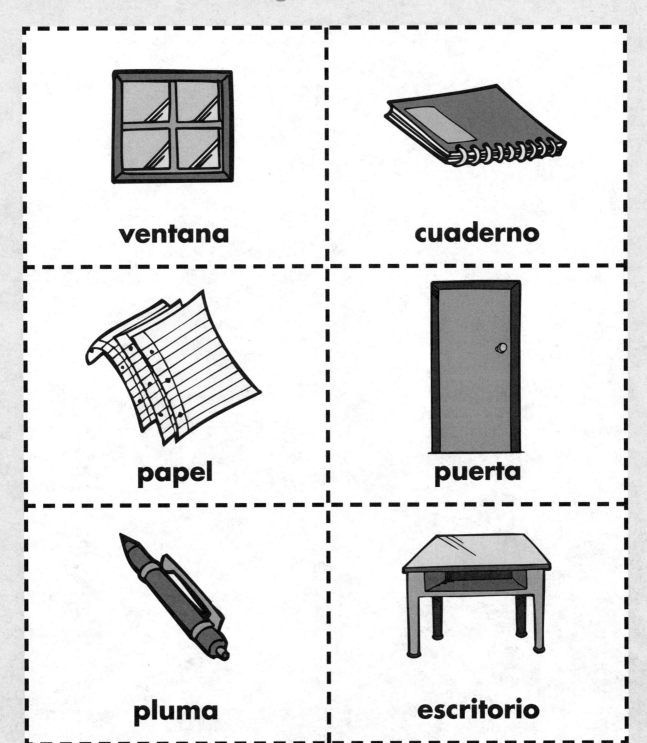

ventana

cuaderno

papel

puerta

pluma

escritorio

Clothing

camisa

pantalones

vestido

calcetines

zapatos

gorro

Clothing

chaqueta

pantalones cortos

botas

guantes

falda

abrigo

Animals

gato

perro

pájaro

pez

pato

culebra

Community

escuela

tienda

museo

biblioteca

casa

parque

Cover Directions

Cut out the 10 covers, one cover per unit.

Me llamo

_____

My

Book

Me llamo

_____

My

Book

Me llamo

My

Book

_____

Me llamo

My

Book

_____

Me llamo

My

Book

_____

Me llamo

My

Book

_____

Me llamo

My

Book

_____

Me llamo

My

Book

_____

Me llamo

My

Book

_____

Me llamo

My

Book

_____

uno

cuatro

dos

cinco

tres

seis

four

one

five

two

six

three

siete	diez
ocho	once
nueve	doce

ten

seven

eleven

eight

twelve

nine

trece

dieciséis

catorce

diecisiete

quince

dieciocho

sixteen	**thirteen**
seventeen	**fourteen**
eighteen	**fifteen**

diecinueve

veintidós

veinte

veintitrés

veintiuno

veinticuatro

twenty-two

nineteen

twenty-three

twenty

twenty-four

twenty-one

veinticinco

las doce

Vamos a contar.

la una

¿Qué hora es?

las dos

twelve o'clock

twenty-five

one o'clock

Let's count.

two o'clock

What time is it?

las tres

las seis

las cuatro

las siete

las cinco

las ocho

six o'clock

three o'clock

seven o'clock

four o'clock

eight o'clock

five o'clock

las nueve	**hora**
las diez	**minuto**
las once	**segundo**

hour

nine o'clock

minute

ten o'clock

second

eleven o'clock

levántense

cierren

siéntense

cállense

abran

pónganse

close

stand up

be quiet

sit down

line up

open

párense

pinten

corten

dibujen

peguen

canten

paint

stop

draw

cut

sing

paste

saquen

contar

mirar

escribir

escuchar

leer

to count

take out

to write

to look

to read

to listen

comer

limpiar

hablar

dormir

beber

tocar

to clean

to eat

to sleep

to speak

to touch

to drink

dar

por favor

hola

gracias

adiós

vengan aquí

please

to give

thank you

hello

come here

goodbye

anden por favor

¿Cómo te llamas?

sí

¿Cómo estás?

¿Hablas español?

¿Qué día es hoy?

What is
your name?

please walk

How are you?

yes

What day
is today?

Do you speak
Spanish?

Estoy bien.

¡Buenos días!

Hoy es lunes.

¡Buenas tardes!

¡Mucho gusto!

¡Buenas noches!

Good morning!

I am fine.

Good afternoon!

Today is Monday.

Good night!

Pleased to meet you!

¡Hasta luego!

miércoles

lunes

jueves

martes

viernes

Wednesday

See you later!

Thursday

Monday

Friday

Tuesday

sábado

febrero

domingo

marzo

enero

abril

February

Saturday

March

Sunday

April

January

mayo

agosto

junio

septiembre

julio

octubre

August

May

September

June

October

July

noviembre

verde

diciembre

anaranjado

rojo

amarillo

green

November

orange

December

yellow

red

azul

blanco

morado

rosado

negro

café

white

blue

pink

purple

brown

black

la camisa

el suéter

los pantalones

la chaqueta

el vestido

los zapatos

sweater

shirt

jacket

pants

shoes

dress

los calcetines

la falda

el gorro

los guantes

las botas

el cinturón

skirt

socks

gloves

cap

belt

boots

la escuela

la clase

el maestro

los alumnos

la maestra

el libro

classroom

school

students

teacher
(male)

book

teacher
(female)

el lápiz

el cuaderno

el papel

las tijeras

el borrador

la pluma

notebook

pencil

scissors

paper

pen

eraser

la salida

el escritorio

el reloj

la mochila

la silla

la regla

desk

exit

backpack

clock

ruler

chair

el crayón

la escritura

la lectura

el inglés

las matemáticas

las ciencias

handwriting

crayon

English

reading

science

math

las ciencias sociales

el rectángulo

el círculo

el triángulo

el cuadrado

el diamante

rectangle

social studies

triangle

circle

diamond

square

GLOSSARY

abeja	bee	*casa*	house
abran	open	*catorce*	fourteen
abrigo	coat	*cero*	zero
abuela	grandmother	*chaqueta*	jacket
abuelo	grandfather	*cierren*	close
adiós	goodbye	*cinco*	five
agua	water	*cine*	movie theater
alegre	happy	*cinturón*	belt
amarillo	yellow	*ciudad*	city
amiga	friend (f)	*cocina*	kitchen
amigo	friend (m)	*comer*	to eat
anaranjado	orange (color)	*contar*	to count
años	years	*corten*	cut
apartamento	apartment	*cuaderno*	notebook
así así	so-so	*cuatro*	four
ayer	yesterday	*cuchara*	spoon
azul	blue	*cuerpo*	body
beber	drink	*dar*	to give
biblioteca	library	*dedo*	finger/toe
bien	well/fine	*día*	day
blanco	white	*dibujen*	draw
blusa	blouse	*diecinueve*	nineteen
boca	mouth	*dieciocho*	eighteen
bonito	pretty	*dieciséis*	sixteen
borrador	eraser	*diecisiete*	seventeen
botas	boots	*dientes*	teeth
brazo	arm	*diez*	ten
caballo	horse	*doce*	twelve
cabeza	head	*domingo*	Sunday
café	brown	*dormir*	to sleep
calcetines	socks	*dormitorio*	bedroom
cama	bed	*dos*	two
camisa	shirt	*ensalada*	salad
canten	sing	*escritorio*	desk
cara	face	*escuela*	school
carne	meat	*estoy*	I am

estómago	stomach	*martes*	Tuesday
falda	skirt	*Me llamo*	My name is
familia	family	*mesa*	table
feo	ugly	*miércoles*	Wednesday
fruta	fruit	*mirar*	to look at
gato	cat	*morado*	purple
gracias	thank you	*museo*	museum
grande	big	*naranja*	orange (fruit)
granja	farm	*nariz*	nose
guantes	gloves	*negro*	black
hablar	to speak	*no*	no
hermana	sister	*noche*	night
hermano	brother	*nueve*	nine
hija	daughter	*nuevo*	new
hijo	son	*ocho*	eight
hola	hello	*ojos*	eyes
hombro	shoulder	*once*	eleven
hoy	today	*orejas*	ears
iglesia	church	*oso*	bear
jueves	Thursday	*padre*	father
jugo	juice	*pájaro*	bird
lámpara	lamp	*pan*	bread
lápiz	pencil	*pantalones*	pants
leche	milk	*pantalones cortos*	shorts
levántense	stand up	*papa*	potato
libro	book	*papel*	paper
limpiar	to clean	*parque*	park
limpio	clean	*pato*	duck
lunes	Monday	*párense*	stop
madre	mother	*peguen*	glue
maestra	teacher (f)	*pelo*	hair
maestro	teacher (m)	*pequeño*	small
mal	bad, not well	*perro*	dog
mano	hand	*pez*	fish
manzana	apple	*pie*	foot
mañana	tomorrow	*pierna*	leg

GLOSSARY

pinten	paint		tío	uncle
plátano	banana		tocar	to touch
pluma	pen		trece	thirteen
pollo	chicken		treinta	thirty
por favor	please		tres	three
primos	cousins		triste	sad
puerta	door		uno	one
queso	cheese		vaca	cow
quince	fifteen		Vamos a contar.	Let's count.
rana	frog		vegetales	vegetables
restaurante	restaurant		veinte	twenty
rodilla	knee		veinticinco	twenty-five
rojo	red		veinticuatro	twenty-four
rosado	pink		veintidós	twenty-two
sala	room		veintinueve	twenty-nine
sandalias	sandals		veintiocho	twenty-eight
sandwich	sandwich		veintiséis	twenty-six
sábado	Saturday		veintisiete	twenty-seven
seis	six		veintitrés	twenty-three
señor	Mr.		veintiuno	twenty-one
señora	Mrs.		ventana	window
señorita	Miss		verde	green
siete	seven		vestido	dress
siéntense	sit down		viejo	old
silla	chair		viernes	Friday
sí	yes		zapatos	shoes
sofá	couch		zoológico	zoo
sombrero	hat		¿Cómo estás?	How are you? (familiar)
sopa	soup		¿Cuántos años tienes?	How old are you? (familiar)
sucio	dirty			
tarde	afternoon		¡Buenas noches!	Good night!
Tengo ___ años.	I am __ years old.		¡Buenas tardes!	Good afternoon!
tienda	store		¡Buenos días!	Good morning!
tienes	you are		¡Hasta luego!	See you later!
tijeras	scissors			
tía	aunt			

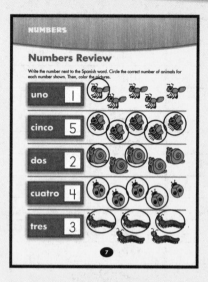

NUMBERS

Numbers Review

Write the number next to the Spanish word. Circle the correct number of animals for each number shown. Then, color the pictures.

uno	1
cinco	5
dos	2
cuatro	4
tres	3

7

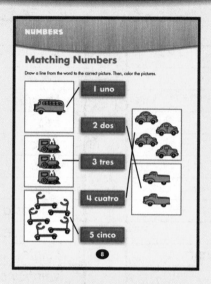

NUMBERS

Matching Numbers

Draw a line from the word to the correct picture. Then, color the pictures.

1 uno
2 dos
3 tres
4 cuatro
5 cinco

8

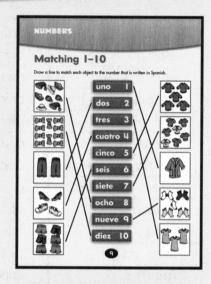

NUMBERS

Matching 1–10

Draw a line to match each object to the number that is written in Spanish.

uno	1
dos	2
tres	3
cuatro	4
cinco	5
seis	6
siete	7
ocho	8
nueve	9
diez	10

9

NUMBERS

Count the Cookies

In each box at the left, write the number that matches the Spanish word. Cross out the correct number of cookies to show the number written in Spanish. The first one is done for you.

2	dos
5	cinco
8	ocho
7	siete
4	cuatro
10	diez
1	uno
9	nueve
6	seis
3	tres

10

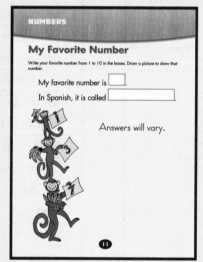

NUMBERS

My Favorite Number

Write your favorite number from 1 to 10 in the boxes. Draw a picture to show that number.

My favorite number is ____

In Spanish, it is called ____

Answers will vary.

11

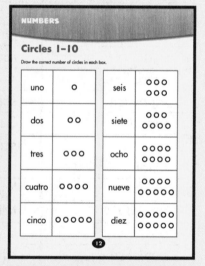

NUMBERS

Circles 1–10

Draw the correct number of circles in each box.

uno	o	seis	ooo / ooo
dos	oo	siete	ooo / oooo
tres	ooo	ocho	oooo / oooo
cuatro	oooo	nueve	oooo / ooooo
cinco	ooooo	diez	ooooo / ooooo

12

NUMBERS

Numbers 0–10

Trace, then write each of the number words from 0 to 10 in Spanish. Use the words at the left to help you.

0	cero	cero	cero
1	uno	uno	uno
2	dos	dos	dos
3	tres	tres	tres
4	cuatro	cuatro	cuatro
5	cinco	cinco	cinco
6	seis	seis	seis
7	siete	siete	siete
8	ocho	ocho	ocho
9	nueve	nueve	nueve
10	diez	diez	diez

13

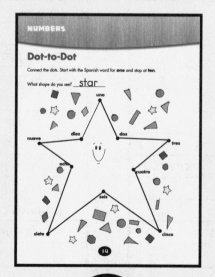

NUMBERS

Dot-to-Dot

Connect the dots. Start with the Spanish word for **one** and stop at **ten**.

What shape do you see? __star__

14

NUMBERS

Numbers 0–20

In the left column, write the number words from 0 to 10 in Spanish. Use the words in the box below to help you. Then, in the second column, write the numbers beside each Spanish word. Two are done for you.

0	cero		11	once
1	uno		12	doce
2	dos		13	trece
3	tres		14	catorce
4	cuatro		15	quince
5	cinco		16	dieciséis
6	seis		17	diecisiete
7	siete		18	dieciocho
8	ocho		19	diecinueve
9	nueve		20	veinte
10	diez			

| siete | uno | nueve | cinco | cuatro | tres |
| ocho | seis | cero | dos | diez | |

15

ANSWER KEY

NUMBERS

Sunshine 0–20

Write the number for each Spanish word. Cross out the correct number of suns to show the number written in Spanish. The first one is done for you.

- quince __15__
- veinte __20__
- tres __3__
- once __11__
- nueve __9__
- trece __13__
- catorce __14__
- dieciocho __18__
- cero __0__
- doce __12__
- My favorite number — Answers will vary.
- seis __6__

16

NUMBERS

Numbers Crossword

Write the Spanish number words in the puzzle spaces. Use the words at the bottom to help you.

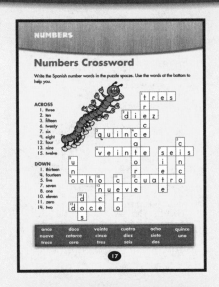

ACROSS
1. three
2. ten
3. fifteen
6. twenty
7. six
9. eight
12. four
13. nine
15. twelve

DOWN
1. thirteen
4. fourteen
5. five
7. seven
8. one
10. eleven
11. zero
14. two

Words: once, doce, veinte, cuatro, ocho, quince, nueve, catorce, cinco, diez, siete, uno, trece, cero, tres, seis, dos

17

NUMBERS

Numbers

After each numeral, write the number word in Spanish. Use the words below to help you.

Words: veinte, cuatro, trece, siete, cinco, dieciséis, doce, once, cero, ocho, seis, catorce, dos, dieciocho, diecisiete, quince, diecinueve, nueve, diez, uno, tres

0	cero	11	once
1	uno	12	doce
2	dos	13	trece
3	tres	14	catorce
4	cuatro	15	quince
5	cinco	16	dieciséis
6	seis	17	diecisiete
7	siete	18	dieciocho
8	ocho	19	diecinueve
9	nueve	20	veinte
10	diez		

18

NUMBERS

Counting On

Follow a pattern to write the numbers from 21–30. Change veinte (20) to veinti and add the number words from uno to nueve. (Watch for accent marks on dos, tres, and seis.) Rewrite the number words from the word bank in order.

Word bank: veintiséis, veinticinco, veintisiete, veintinueve, veintiocho, veintidós, veintiuno, treinta, veintitrés, veinticuatro

21	veintiuno	26	veintiséis
22	veintidós	27	veintisiete
23	veintitrés	28	veintiocho
24	veinticuatro	29	veintinueve
25	veinticinco	30	treinta

Complete the pattern to write the numbers from 31–39. Use the Spanish word y (and) to join treinta (30) with the number words uno to nueve. One is done for you.

31	treinta y uno	36	treinta y seis
32	treinta y dos	37	treinta y siete
33	treinta y tres	38	treinta y ocho
34	treinta y cuatro	39	treinta y nueve
35	treinta y cinco		

19

NUMBERS

Number Find

Circle the Spanish number words that you find in the word search. Then, write the English meaning of each word. Words can be across, down, diagonal, or backward.

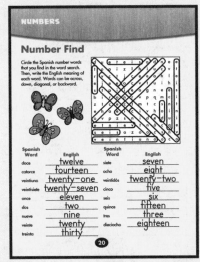

Spanish Word	English	Spanish Word	English
doce	twelve	siete	seven
catorce	fourteen	ocho	eight
veintiuno	twenty-one	veintidós	twenty-two
veintisiete	twenty-seven	cinco	five
once	eleven	seis	six
dos	two	quince	fifteen
nueve	nine	tres	three
veinte	twenty	dieciocho	eighteen
treinta	thirty		

20

NUMBERS

Counting by Tens

The Spanish numbers ten, twenty, thirty, forty, and fifty are written out of order below. Write the value of each number word in the blank.

- __30__ treinta
- __50__ cincuenta
- __40__ cuarenta
- __10__ diez
- __20__ veinte

Write the numbers 30–59 in Spanish. Numbers 41–59 follow the same pattern as numbers 31–39.

30	treinta	45	cuarenta y cinco
31	treinta y uno	46	cuarenta y seis
32	treinta y dos	47	cuarenta y siete
33	treinta y tres	48	cuarenta y ocho
34	treinta y cuatro	49	cuarenta y nueve
35	treinta y cinco	50	cincuenta
36	treinta y seis	51	cincuenta y uno
37	treinta y siete	52	cincuenta y dos
38	treinta y ocho	53	cincuenta y tres
39	treinta y nueve	54	cincuenta y cuatro
40	cuarenta	55	cincuenta y cinco
41	cuarenta y uno	56	cincuenta y seis
42	cuarenta y dos	57	cincuenta y siete
43	cuarenta y tres	58	cincuenta y ocho
44	cuarenta y cuatro	59	cincuenta y nueve

21

ALPHABET

Listening Practice

Say the Spanish word for each number out loud. Write the first letter of the words you hear.

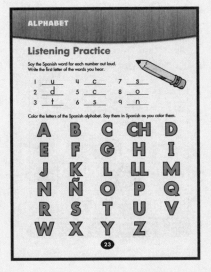

- 1. u
- 2. d
- 3. t
- 4. c
- 5. c
- 6. c
- 7. s
- 8. o

Color the letters of the Spanish alphabet. Say them in Spanish as you color them.

A B CH D E F G H I J K L LL M N Ñ O P Q R S T U V W X Y Z

23

ALPHABET

The Alphabet

El abecedario (the alphabet)

a	a	h	hache	ñ	eñe	v	ve
b	be	i	i	o	o	w	doble ve
c	ce	j	jota	p	pe	x	equis
ch	che	k	ka	q	cu	y	i griego
d	de	l	ele	r	ere	z	zeta
e	e	ll	elle	s	ese		
f	efe	m	eme	t	te		
g	ge	n	ene	u	u		

Listening Practice

Write each letter of the alphabet as you say it out loud.

- 1. a
- 2. b
- 3. c
- 4. ch
- 5. d
- 6. e
- 7. f
- 8. g
- 9. h
- 10. i
- 11. j
- 12. k
- 13. l
- 14. ll
- 15. m
- 16. n
- 17. ñ
- 18. o
- 19. p
- 20. q
- 21. r
- 22. s
- 23. t
- 24. u
- 25. v
- 26. w
- 27. x
- 28. y
- 29. z

24

PARTS OF SPEECH

Using You

Spanish uses two different forms of the pronoun you.

Tú is used when talking to
1. someone you refer to by a first name.
2. your sister, brother, or cousin.
3. a classmate.
4. a close friend.
5. a child younger than yourself.

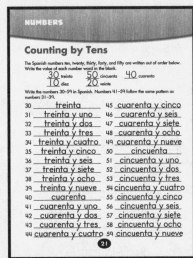

Usted (Ud.) is used when talking to
1. someone with a title.
2. an older person.
3. a stranger.
4. a person of authority.

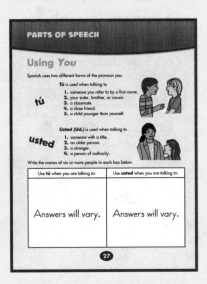

Write the names of six or more people in each box below.

Use tú when you are talking to:	Use usted when you are talking to:
Answers will vary.	Answers will vary.

27

ANSWER KEY

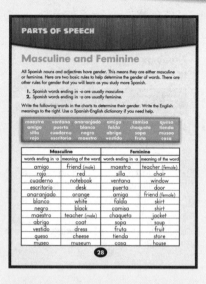

PARTS OF SPEECH

Masculine and Feminine

All Spanish nouns and adjectives have gender. This means they are either masculine or feminine. Here are two basic rules to help determine the gender of words. There are other rules for gender that you will learn as you study more Spanish.

1. Spanish words ending in -o are usually masculine.
2. Spanish words ending in -a are usually feminine.

Write the following words in the charts to determine their gender. Write the English meanings to the right. Use a Spanish-English dictionary if you need help.

maestra	ventana	anaranjado	amiga	camisa	queso
amigo	puerta	blanco	falda	chaqueta	tienda
silla	cuaderno	negro	abrigo	sopa	museo
rojo	escritorio	maestro	vestido	fruta	casa

Masculine		Feminine	
words ending in -o	meaning of the word	words ending in -a	meaning of the word
amigo	friend (male)	maestra	teacher (female)
rojo	red	silla	chair
cuaderno	notebook	ventana	window
escritorio	desk	puerta	door
anaranjado	orange	amiga	friend (female)
blanco	white	falda	skirt
negro	black	camisa	shirt
maestro	teacher (male)	chaqueta	jacket
abrigo	coat	sopa	soup
vestido	dress	fruta	fruit
queso	cheese	tienda	store
museo	museum	casa	house

28

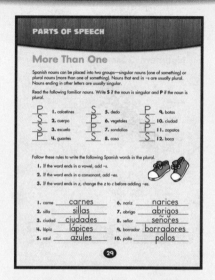

PARTS OF SPEECH

More Than One

Spanish nouns can be placed into two groups—singular nouns (one of something) or plural nouns (more than one of something). Nouns that end in -s are usually plural. Nouns ending in other letters are usually singular.

Read the following familiar nouns. Write **S** if the noun is singular and **P** if the noun is plural.

P 1. calcetines
S 2. cuerpo
S 3. escuela
P 4. guantes
S 5. dedo
P 6. vegetales
P 7. sandalias
S 8. casa
P 9. botas
S 10. ciudad
P 11. zapatos
S 12. boca

Follow these rules to write the following Spanish words in the plural.

1. If the word ends in a vowel, add -s.
2. If the word ends in a consonant, add -es.
3. If the word ends in z, change the z to c before adding -es.

1. carne ___carnes___
2. silla ___sillas___
3. ciudad ___ciudades___
4. lápiz ___lápices___
5. azul ___azules___
6. nariz ___narices___
7. abrigo ___abrigos___
8. señor ___señores___
9. borrador ___borradores___
10. pollo ___pollos___

29

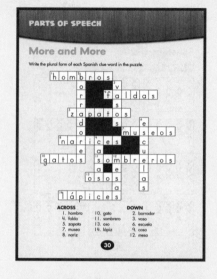

PARTS OF SPEECH

More and More

Write the plural form of each Spanish clue word in the puzzle.

(crossword puzzle with answers: hombros, faldas, zapatos, museos, narices, gatos, sombreros, osos, lápices)

ACROSS
1. hombro
4. falda
5. zapato
7. museo
8. nariz
10. gato
11. sombrero
13. oso
14. lápiz

DOWN
2. borrador
3. vaso
6. escuela
9. casa
12. mesa

30

PARTS OF SPEECH

It's a Small World

In Spanish, there are four ways to say "the"—el, la, los, and las. The definite article (the) agrees with its noun in gender (masculine or feminine) and number (singular or plural).

Masculine singular nouns go with el. Feminine singular nouns go with la.

Examples: el libro (the book)   el papel (the paper)
la silla (the chair)   la regla (the ruler)

Masculine plural nouns go with los. Feminine plural nouns go with las.

Examples: los libros (the books)   los papeles (the papers)
las sillas (the chairs)   las reglas (the rulers)

Refer to the word bank to complete the chart. Write the singular and plural forms and the correct definite articles. Two have been done for you.

| cuaderno | mesa | pluma | oso | falda |
| papel | gato | bota | silla | libro |

English	Masculine Singular	Masculine Plural
the book	el libro	los libros
the paper	el papel	los papeles
the notebook	el cuaderno	los cuadernos
the cat	el gato	los gatos
the bear	el oso	los osos

English	Feminine Singular	Feminine Plural
the chair	la silla	las sillas
the table	la mesa	las mesas
the boot	la bota	las botas
the skirt	la falda	las faldas
the pen	la pluma	las plumas

31

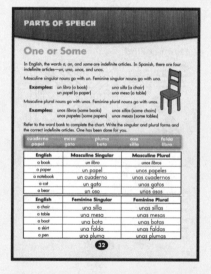

PARTS OF SPEECH

One or Some

In English, the words a, an, and some are indefinite articles. In Spanish, there are four indefinite articles—un, una, unas, and unos.

Masculine singular nouns go with un. Feminine singular nouns go with una.

Examples: un libro (a book)   una silla (a chair)
un papel (a paper)   una mesa (a table)

Masculine plural nouns go with unos. Feminine plural nouns go with unas.

Examples: unos libros (some books)   unas sillas (some chairs)
unos papeles (some papers)   unas mesas (some tables)

Refer to the word bank to complete the chart. Write the singular and plural forms and the correct indefinite articles. One has been done for you.

| cuaderno | mesa | pluma | oso | falda |
| papel | gato | bota | silla | libro |

English	Masculine Singular	Masculine Plural
a book	un libro	unos libros
a paper	un papel	unos papeles
a notebook	un cuaderno	unos cuadernos
a cat	un gato	unos gatos
a bear	un oso	unos osos

English	Feminine Singular	Feminine Plural
a chair	una silla	unas sillas
a table	una mesa	unas mesas
a boot	una bota	unas botas
a skirt	una falda	unas faldas
a pen	una pluma	unas plumas

32

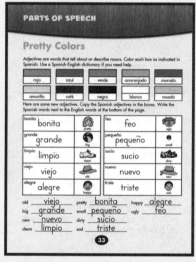

PARTS OF SPEECH

Pretty Colors

Adjectives are words that tell about or describe nouns. Color each box as indicated in Spanish. Use a Spanish-English dictionary if you need help.

| rojo | azul | verde | anaranjado | morado |
| amarillo | café | negro | blanco | rosado |

Here are some new adjectives. Copy the Spanish adjectives in the boxes. Write the Spanish words next to the English words at the bottom of the page.

bonita	bonita	feo	feo
grande	grande	pequeño	pequeño
limpio	limpio	sucio	sucio
viejo	viejo	nuevo	nuevo
alegre	alegre	triste	triste

old ___viejo___   pretty ___bonita___   happy ___alegre___
big ___grande___   small ___pequeño___   ugly ___feo___
new ___nuevo___   dirty ___sucio___
clean ___limpio___   sad ___triste___

33

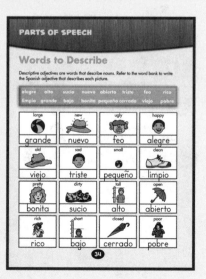

PARTS OF SPEECH

Words to Describe

Descriptive adjectives are words that describe nouns. Refer to the word bank to write the Spanish adjective that describes each picture.

| alegre | alto | sucio | nuevo | abierto | triste | feo | rico |
| limpio | grande | bajo | bonita | pequeño | cerrado | viejo | pobre |

large	new	ugly	happy
grande	nuevo	feo	alegre
old	sad	small	clean
viejo	triste	pequeño	limpio
pretty	dirty	tall	open
bonita	sucio	alto	abierto
rich	short	closed	poor
rico	bajo	cerrado	pobre

34

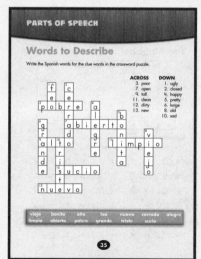

PARTS OF SPEECH

Words to Describe

Write the Spanish words for the clue words in the crossword puzzle.

ACROSS
3. poor
7. open
9. tall
11. clean
12. dirty
13. new

DOWN
1. ugly
2. closed
4. happy
5. pretty
6. large
8. old
10. sad

(crossword with answers: pobre, abierto, alto, limpio, sucio, nuevo)

| viejo | bonita | alto | feo | nuevo | cerrado | alegre |
| limpio | abierto | pobre | grande | triste | sucio |

35

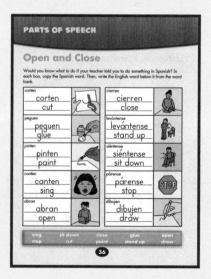

PARTS OF SPEECH

Open and Close

Would you know what to do if your teacher told you to do something in Spanish? In each box, copy the Spanish word. Then, write the English word below it from the word bank.

corten	corten / cut	cierren	cierren / close
peguen	peguen / glue	levántense	levántense / stand up
pinten	pinten / paint	siéntense	siéntense / sit down
canten	canten / sing	párense	párense / stop
abran	abran / open	dibujen	dibujen / draw

| sing | sit down | close | glue | open |
| stop | cut | point | stand up | draw |

36

248

ANSWER KEY

Action Words

In each box, copy the Spanish action verbs. Then, write the English word below it.

comer	hablar
comer to eat	hablar to speak
beber	limpiar
beber to drink	limpiar to clean
dormir	mirar
dormir to sleep	mirar to look at
tocar	dar
tocar to touch	dar to give

to touch	to look at	to eat	to give
to drink	to speak	to clean	to sleep

38

First Sentences

Create original sentences in Spanish using these sentence starters and the verbs in the word bank. You may use one sentence starter more than once. Write the English meanings on the lines below the Spanish.

comer	beber	dormir	tocar
hablar	limpiar	mirar	dar

Sentence Starters

Me gusta _____.	(I like _____.)
No me gusta _____.	(I don't like _____.)
Quiero _____.	(I want _____.)
Necesito _____.	(I need _____.)

1. Answers will vary.
2.
3.
4.
5.

39

Action Words

Refer to the word bank to write the Spanish word that matches each picture.

comer	estudiar	limpiar	mirar	jugar	dar
hablar	beber	dormir	trabajar	tocar	ir

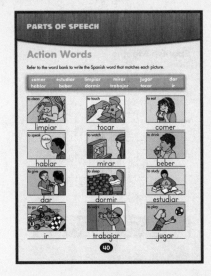

to clean	to touch	to eat
limpiar	tocar	comer
to speak	to watch	to drink
hablar	mirar	beber
to give	to sleep	to study
dar	dormir	estudiar
to go	to work	to play
ir	trabajar	jugar

40

Capitals

Spanish uses capital letters less often than the English language. Follow these rules as your guide.

Capitalization Rules

1. All Spanish sentences begin with capital letters.
2. Names of people begin with capital letters.
3. Names of places (cities, regions, countries, and continents) and holidays begin with capital letters.
4. Titles are not capitalized unless abbreviated (señor→Sr., usted→Ud.).
5. Some words that are normally capitalized in English may not be capitalized in Spanish (nationalities, religions, languages, months, and days).

Write **sí** if the word should be capitalized. Write **no** if it should remain lowercase.

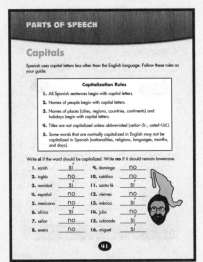

1. sarah	sí	9. domingo	no
2. inglés	no	10. católico	no
3. navidad	sí	11. santa fé	sí
4. español	no	12. viernes	no
5. mexicano	no	13. méxico	sí
6. africa	sí	14. julio	no
7. señor	no	15. colorado	sí
8. enero	no	16. miguel	sí

41

Introductions Review

Say each expression out loud. Circle the picture that tells the meaning of each word.

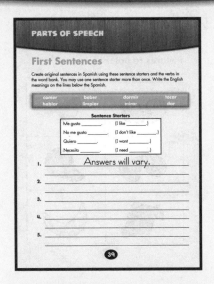

| gracias |
| Tengo seis años. |
| por favor |
| amigo |
| amigos |
| ¡Hasta luego! |
| amiga |
| sí |

46

Greetings

Write the English meaning of the Spanish words and phrases.

1. señor — Mr.
2. señora — Mrs.
3. señorita — Miss
4. maestro — teacher (male)
5. maestra — teacher (female)
6. ¡Buenos días! — Good morning!
7. ¡Buenas tardes! — Good afternoon!
8. ¡Buenas noches! — Good night!
9. Vamos a contar. — Let's count.

Mr.	Good night!	Good morning!
Good afternoon!	teacher (female)	teacher (male)
Miss	Let's count.	Mrs.

Draw a picture to show the time of day that you use each expression.

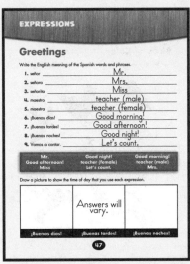

	Answers will vary.	
¡Buenos días!	¡Buenas tardes!	¡Buenas noches!

47

Greetings

Refer to the word bank to translate the Spanish greetings, questions, and answers.

¡Buenos días!	Good morning!
¡Buenas tardes!	Good afternoon!
¡Buenas noches!	Good night!
¿Cómo estás?	How are you?
bien, gracias	fine, thank you
mal	not well
así, así	ok/so-so
¿Cómo te llamas?	What is your name?
Me llamo ___	My name is ___.
¿Cuántos años tienes?	How old are you?
Tengo ___ años.	I am ___ years old.
adiós	goodbye
hola	hello

goodbye	Good morning!	I am ___ years old.
fine, thank you	Good afternoon!	
	hello	How old are you?
	What is your name?	My name is ___.
	not well	
	ok/so-so	
	Good night!	

teacher (m/f)	Miss	no
Mr.	friend (m/f)	please
Mrs.	yes	

Refer to the word bank to translate the Spanish vocabulary.

amigo/amiga	friend (m/f)
sí	yes
no	no
por favor	please
señor	Mr.
señora	Mrs.
maestro/maestra	teacher (m/f)
señorita	Miss

48

Yesterday and Today

Write the Spanish words for the days of the week. Remember, in Spanish-speaking countries, Monday is the first day of the week.

miércoles	jueves	domingo	martes
viernes	lunes	sábado	

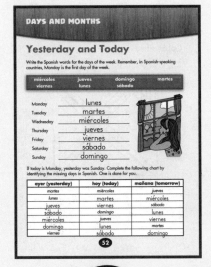

Monday	lunes
Tuesday	martes
Wednesday	miércoles
Thursday	jueves
Friday	viernes
Saturday	sábado
Sunday	domingo

If today is Monday, yesterday was Sunday. Complete the following chart by identifying the missing days in Spanish. One is done for you.

ayer (yesterday)	hoy (today)	mañana (tomorrow)
martes	miércoles	jueves
lunes	martes	miércoles
jueves	viernes	sábado
sábado	domingo	lunes
miércoles	jueves	viernes
domingo	lunes	martes
viernes	sábado	domingo

52

Writing Practice

Copy the following paragraph in your best handwriting. Practice reading it out loud.

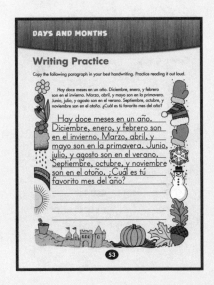

Hay doce meses en un año. Diciembre, enero, y febrero son en el invierno. Marzo, abril, y mayo son en la primavera. Junio, julio, y agosto son en el verano. Septiembre, octubre, y noviembre son en el otoño. ¿Cuál es tú favorito mes del año?

Hay doce meses en un año. Diciembre, enero, y febrero son en el invierno. Marzo, abril, y mayo son en la primavera. Junio, julio, y agosto son en el verano. Septiembre, octubre, y noviembre son en el otoño. ¿Cuál es tú favorito mes del año?

53

DAYS AND MONTHS

Spanish Months

Write the Spanish word for the clue words in the crossword puzzle.

ACROSS
4. July
9. May
10. September
11. June
12. January

DOWN
1. April
2. November
3. December
5. March
6. February
7. August
8. October

marzo | mayo | diciembre | junio
septiembre | octubre | julio | agosto
abril | enero | febrero | noviembre

54

COLORS

Pictures to Color

Color the pictures according to each color word.

rojo	azul
verde	anaranjado
morado	amarillo

57

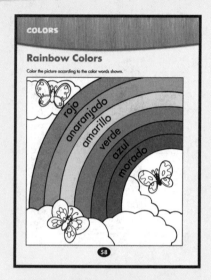

COLORS

Rainbow Colors

Color the picture according to the color words shown.

rojo
anaranjado
amarillo
verde
azul
morado

58

COLORS

Birds of Color

Color the birds according to the words listed.

azul
café
morado
rojo
rosado
verde
negro
amarillo
anaranjado

59

COLORS

Color Search

Cut out pictures from a magazine that match the colors below. Glue each picture next to the correct color word. Answers will vary.

rojo	amarillo
azul	café
verde	negro
anaranjado	blanco
morado	rosado

60

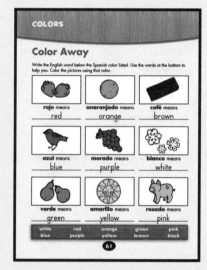

COLORS

Color Away

Write the English word below the Spanish color listed. Use the words at the bottom to help you. Color the pictures using that color.

rojo means red | **anaranjado** means orange | **café** means brown
azul means blue | **morado** means purple | **blanco** means white
verde means green | **amarillo** means yellow | **rosado** means pink

white | red | orange | green | pink
blue | purple | yellow | brown | black

61

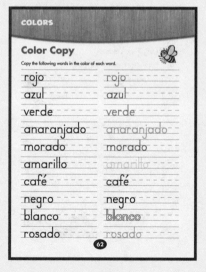

COLORS

Color Copy

Copy the following words in the color of each word.

rojo — rojo
azul — azul
verde — verde
anaranjado — anaranjado
morado — morado
amarillo — amarillo
café — café
negro — negro
blanco — blanco
rosado — rosado

62

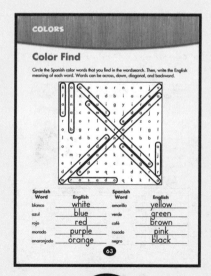

COLORS

Color Find

Circle the Spanish color words that you find in the wordsearch. Then, write the English meaning of each word. Words can be across, diagonal, and backward.

Spanish Word	English	Spanish Word	English
blanco	white	amarillo	yellow
azul	blue	verde	green
rojo	red	café	brown
morado	purple	rosado	pink
anaranjado	orange	negro	black

63

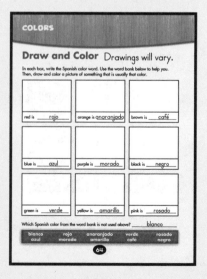

COLORS

Draw and Color Drawings will vary.

In each box, write the Spanish color word. Use the word bank below to help you. Then, draw and color a picture of something that is usually that color.

red is rojo	orange is anaranjado	brown is café
blue is azul	purple is morado	black is negro
green is verde	yellow is amarillo	pink is rosado

Which Spanish color from the word bank is not used above? __blanco__

blanco | rojo | anaranjado | verde | rosado
azul | morado | amarillo | cafe | negro

64

ANSWER KEY

COLORS

Across the Spectrum

Write the Spanish for each clue word in the crossword puzzle.

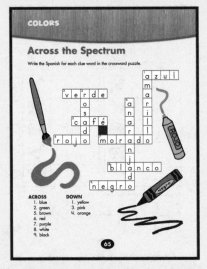

ACROSS
1. blue
2. green
5. brown
6. red
7. purple
8. white
9. black

DOWN
1. yellow
3. pink
4. orange

65

FOOD

Food Meanings

Say each word out loud. Circle the picture that shows the meaning of each word.

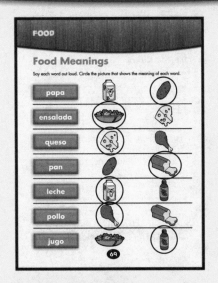

papa
ensalada
queso
pan
leche
pollo
jugo

69

FOOD

Food Words

Say each word out loud. Write the English word next to it.

pollo __chicken__   papa __potato__   queso __cheese__

pan __bread__

leche __milk__   ensalada __salad__   jugo __juice__

Color the blocks with letters.
Do not color the blocks with numbers. What word did you find? __leche__

70

FOOD

Food Riddles

Answer the riddles. Use the size and shape of the word blocks along with the answers at the bottom to help you.

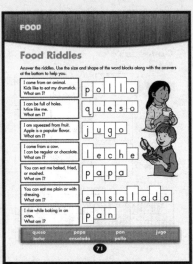

I come from an animal. Kids like to eat my drumstick. What am I? — p o l l o

I can be full of holes. Mice love me. What am I? — q u e s o

I am squeezed from fruit. Apple is a popular flavor. What am I? — j u g o

I come from a cow. I can be regular or chocolate. What am I? — l e c h e

You can eat me baked, fried, or mashed. What am I? — p a p a

You can eat me plain or with dressing. What am I? — e n s a l a d a

I rise while baking in an oven. What am I? — p a n

| queso | papa | pan | jugo |
| leche | ensalada | pollo | |

71

FOOD

New Food Words

Say each word out loud. Copy each word and color the picture.

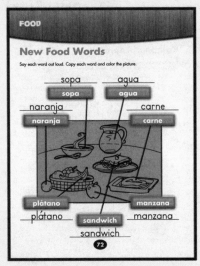

sopa — sopa
agua — agua
naranja — naranja
carne — carne
plátano — plátano
sandwich — sandwich
manzana — manzana

72

FOOD

A Square Meal

Refer to the word bank to write the name of each food in Spanish.

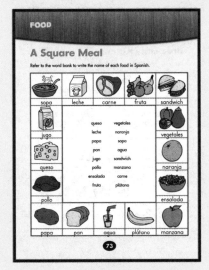

| sopa | leche | carne | fruta | sandwich |

jugo				vegetales
	queso	vegetales		
	leche	naranja		naranja
queso	papa	sopa		
	pan	agua		
pollo	jugo	sandwich		ensalada
	ensalada	manzana		
	fruta	plátano		

| papa | pan | agua | plátano | manzana |

73

FOOD

Searching for Food

Circle the Spanish words that you find in the wordsearch. Then, write the English meaning of each word. Words can be across, down, diagonal, or backward.

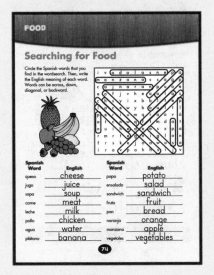

Spanish Word	English	Spanish Word	English
queso	cheese	papa	potato
jugo	juice	ensalada	salad
sopa	soup	sandwich	sandwich
carne	meat	fruta	fruit
leche	milk	pan	bread
pollo	chicken	naranja	orange
agua	water	manzana	apple
plátano	banana	vegetales	vegetables

74

FOOD

Eat It Up

Write the Spanish for the clue words in the crossword puzzle.

ACROSS
4. sandwich
6. vegetables
8. banana
10. bread
12. orange
13. potato
15. water
16. juice

DOWN
1. milk
2. fruit
3. apple
5. chicken
7. salad
9. meat
11. soup
14. cheese

ensalada	sandwich	sopa	fruta	papa	pollo
pan	plátano	leche	jugo	queso	
carne	naranja	manzana	agua	vegetales	

75

ANIMALS

Animal Art   Answers will vary.

Choose four animals and draw each animal in its home. Label it with the Spanish animal word.

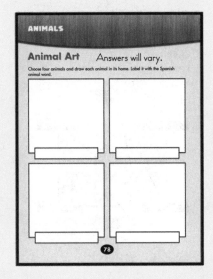

78

251

ANSWER KEY

ANIMALS
Animal Crossword
Use the picture clues to complete the puzzle. Choose from the Spanish words at the bottom of the page.

Crossword answers:
- p, gato, pájaro
- culebra
- perro, r, r
- pato
- pez, z

gato	perro	pájaro
pez	pato	culebra

79

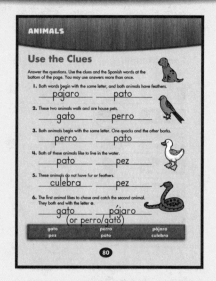

ANIMALS
Use the Clues
Answer the questions. Use the clues and the Spanish words at the bottom of the page. You may use answers more than once.

1. Both words begin with the same letter, and both animals have feathers.
   pájaro   pato
2. These two animals walk and are house pets.
   gato   perro
3. Both animals begin with the same letter. One quacks and the other barks.
   perro   pato
4. Both of these animals like to live in the water.
   pato   pez
5. These animals do not have fur or feathers.
   culebra   pez
6. The first animal likes to chase and catch the second animal. They both end with the letter o.
   gato   pájaro
   (or perro/gato)

gato	perro	pájaro
pez	pato	culebra

80

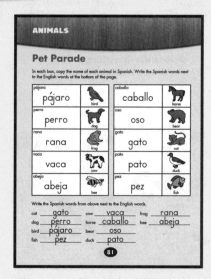

ANIMALS
Pet Parade
In each box, copy the name of each animal in Spanish. Write the Spanish words next to the English words at the bottom of the page.

pájaro	bird	caballo	horse
perro	dog	oso	bear
rana	frog	gato	cat
vaca	cow	pato	duck
abeja	bee	pez	fish

Write the Spanish words from above next to the English words.

cat gato   cow vaca   frog rana
dog perro   horse caballo   bee abeja
bird pájaro bear oso
fish pez   duck pato

81

ANIMALS
Three Little Kittens
Draw a picture to match the Spanish phrase in each box.

seis pájaros	cuatro perros
nueve abejas	siete osos
tres gatos	dos vacas
cinco patos	ocho caballos
diez ranas	un pez

82

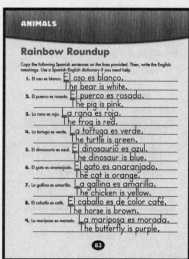

ANIMALS
Rainbow Roundup
Copy the following Spanish sentences on the lines provided. Then, write the English meanings. Use a Spanish-English dictionary if you need help.

1. El oso es blanco.
   El oso es blanco.
   The bear is white.
2. El puerco es rosado.
   El puerco es rosado.
   The pig is pink.
3. La rana es roja.
   La rana es roja.
   The frog is red.
4. La tortuga es verde.
   La tortuga es verde.
   The turtle is green.
5. El dinosaurio es azul.
   El dinosaurio es azul.
   The dinosaur is blue.
6. El gato es anaranjado.
   El gato es anaranjado.
   The cat is orange.
7. La gallina es amarilla.
   La gallina es amarilla.
   The chicken is yellow.
8. El caballo es café.
   El caballo es de color café.
   The horse is brown.
9. La mariposa es morada.
   La mariposa es morada.
   The butterfly is purple.

83

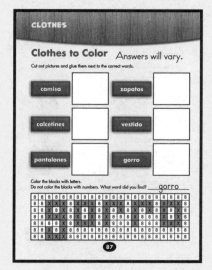

CLOTHES
Clothes to Color   Answers will vary.
Cut out pictures and glue them next to the correct words.

camisa   zapatos
calcetines   vestido
pantalones   gorro

Color the blocks with letters.
Do not color the blocks with numbers. What word did you find?   gorro

87

CLOTHES
Clothing
Say each word out loud. Copy each word and color the picture.

pantalones
pantalones
gorro   vestido
gorro   vestido
camisa   zapatos
camisa   zapatos
calcetines
calcetines

88

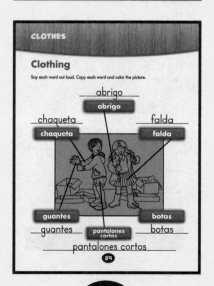

CLOTHES
Clothing
Say each word out loud. Copy each word and color the picture.

abrigo
abrigo
chaqueta   falda
chaqueta   falda
guantes   botas
guantes   botas
pantalones cortos
pantalones cortos

89

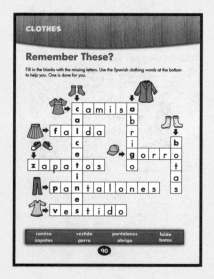

CLOTHES
Remember These?
Fill in the blanks with the missing letters. Use the Spanish clothing words at the bottom to help you. One is done for you.

Crossword answers:
- camisa
- falda, a, c, e
- zapatos, t, g, orro, a, s
- pantalones
- vestido
- b, r, i, g, o
- b, o, t, a, s

camisa	vestido	pantalones	falda
zapatos	gorro	abrigo	botas

90

252

ANSWER KEY

Clothes Closet

Refer to the word bank and write the Spanish word for each item of clothing pictured.

vestido	calcetines	botas	zapatos
sombrero	cinturón	falda	chaqueta
guantes	pantalones cortos	pantalones	camisa

shirt	camisa	pants	pantalones
shorts	pantalones cortos	hat	sombrero
socks	calcetines	skirt	falda
shoes	zapatos	belt	cinturón
boots	botas	dress	vestido
gloves	guantes	jacket	chaqueta

91

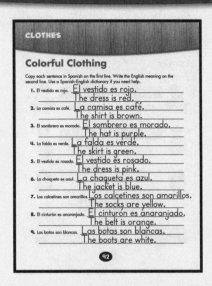

Colorful Clothing

Copy each sentence in Spanish on the first line. Write the English meaning on the second line. Use a Spanish-English dictionary if you need help.

1. El vestido es rojo. El vestido es rojo.
   The dress is red.
2. La camisa es café. La camisa es café.
   The shirt is brown.
3. El sombrero es morado. El sombrero es morado.
   The hat is purple.
4. La falda es verde. La falda es verde.
   The skirt is green.
5. El vestido es rosado. El vestido es rosado.
   The dress is pink.
6. La chaqueta es azul. La chaqueta es azul.
   The jacket is blue.
7. Los calcetines son amarillos. Los calcetines son amarillos.
   The socks are yellow.
8. El cinturón es anaranjado. El cinturón es anaranjado.
   The belt is orange.
9. Las botas son blancas. Las botas son blancas.
   The boots are white.

92

Clothes Closet

Circle the Spanish words that you find in the puzzle. Write the English meanings at the bottom of the page next to the Spanish words from the puzzle.

Spanish Word	English	Spanish Word	English
abrigo	coat	sandalias	sandals
guantes	gloves	calcetines	socks
blusa	blouse	falda	skirt
chaqueta	jacket	vestido	dress
pantalones	pants	camisa	shirt
botas	boots	gorro	cap
cinturón	belt	zapatos	shoes

93

What's on Your Face?

Say each word out loud. Copy each word.

pelo — pelo
nariz — nariz
ojos — ojos
orejas — orejas
dientes — dientes
boca — boca
cara — cara

96

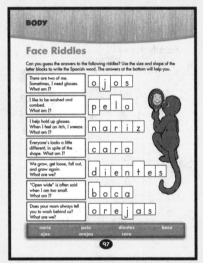

Face Riddles

Can you guess the answers to the following riddles? Use the size and shape of the letter blocks to write the Spanish word. The answers at the bottom will help you.

There are two of me. Sometimes, I need glasses. What am I? — ojos

I like to be washed and combed. What am I? — pelo

I help hold up glasses. When I feel an itch, I sneeze. What am I? — nariz

Everyone's looks a little different, in spite of the shape. What am I? — cara

We grow, get loose, fall out, and grow again. What are we? — dientes

"Open wide" is often said when I am too small. What am I? — boca

Does your mom always tell you to wash behind us? What are we? — orejas

| nariz | pelo | dientes | boca |
| ojos | orejas | cara | |

97

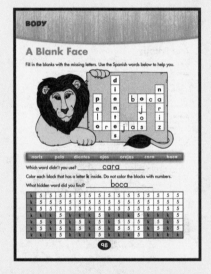

A Blank Face

Fill in the blanks with the missing letters. Use the Spanish words below to help you.

| nariz | pelo | dientes | ojos | orejas | cara | boca |

Which word didn't you use? cara

Color each block that has a letter k inside. Do not color the blocks with numbers.

What hidden word did you find? boca

98

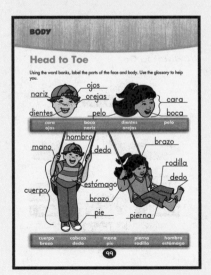

Head to Toe

Using the word banks, label the parts of the face and body. Use the glossary to help you.

nariz, ojos, orejas, dientes, pelo, cara, boca

| cara | boca | dientes | pelo |
| ojos | nariz | orejas | |

hombro, mano, dedo, brazo, rodilla, dedo, cuerpo, estómago, brazo, pie, pierna

| cuerpo | cabeza | mano | pierna | hombro |
| brazo | dedo | pie | rodilla | estómago |

99

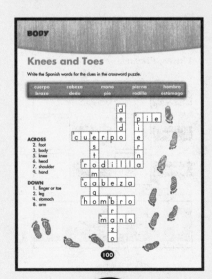

Knees and Toes

Write the Spanish words for the clues in the crossword puzzle.

| cuerpo | cabeza | mano | pierna | hombro |
| brazo | dedo | pie | rodilla | estómago |

ACROSS
3. foot
4. body
5. knee
6. head
7. shoulder
9. hand

DOWN
1. finger or toe
2. leg
4. stomach
8. arm

Across: cuerpo, rodilla, cabeza, hombro, mano
Down: dedo, pie, pierna, estómago, brazo

100

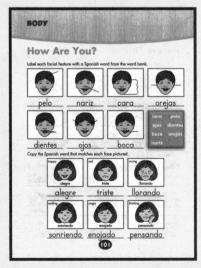

How Are You?

Label each facial feature with a Spanish word from the word bank.

pelo, nariz, cara, orejas, dientes, ojos, boca

cara	pelo
ojos	dientes
boca	orejas
nariz	

Copy the Spanish word that matches each face pictured.

| happy alegre | sad triste | crying llorando |
| smiling sonriendo | angry enojado | thinking pensando |

101

253

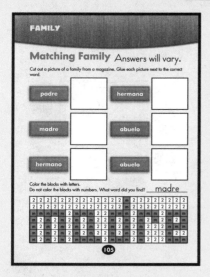

FAMILY

Matching Family — Answers will vary.

Cut out a picture of a family from a magazine. Glue each picture next to the correct word.

padre | hermana
madre | abuelo
hermano | abuelo

Color the blocks with letters.
Do not color the blocks with numbers. What word did you find? __madre__

105

FAMILY

Family

Copy each word and color the pictures.

madre — madre
padre — padre
abuelo — abuelo
abuela — abuela
hermana — hermana
hermano — hermano

Let's learn two new words.

chico — chico
chica — chica

106

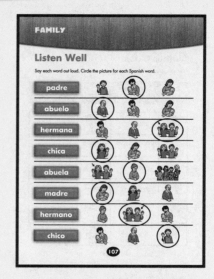

FAMILY

Listen Well

Say each word out loud. Circle the picture for each Spanish word.

padre
abuelo
hermana
chica
abuela
madre
hermano
chico

107

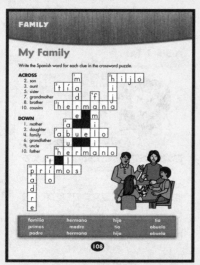

FAMILY

My Family

Write the Spanish word for each clue in the crossword puzzle.

ACROSS
2. son
3. aunt
5. sister
7. grandmother
8. brother
10. cousins

DOWN
1. mother
2. daughter
4. family
6. grandfather
9. uncle
10. father

familia | hermano | hijo | tia
primos | madre | tia | abuelo
padre | hermana | hija | abuela

108

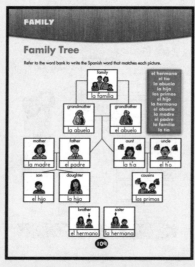

FAMILY

Family Tree

Refer to the word bank to write the Spanish word that matches each picture.

family — la familia
grandmother — la abuela
grandfather — el abuelo
mother — la madre
father — el padre
aunt — la tía
uncle — el tío
son — el hijo
daughter — la hija
cousins — los primos
brother — el hermano
sister — la hermana

el hermano
el tío
la abuela
los primos
el hijo
la hermana
el abuelo
la madre
el padre
la familia
la tía

109

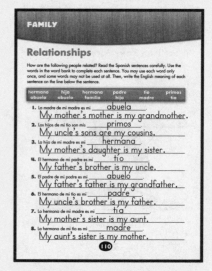

FAMILY

Relationships

How are the following people related? Read the Spanish sentences carefully. Use the words in the word bank to complete each sentence. You may use each word only once, and some words may not be used at all. Then, write the English meaning of each sentence on the line below the sentence.

hermana | hija | hermana | padre | tio | primos
abuela | abuelo | familia | hijo | madre | tia

1. La madre de mi madre es mi __abuela__
   My mother's mother is my grandmother.
2. Los hijos de mi tío son mis __primos__
   My uncle's sons are my cousins.
3. La hija de mi madre es mi __hermana__
   My mother's daughter is my sister.
4. El hermano de mi padre es mi __tio__
   My father's brother is my uncle.
5. El padre de mi padre es mi __abuelo__
   My father's father is my grandfather.
6. El hermano de mi tío es mi __padre__
   My uncle's brother is my father.
7. La hermana de mi madre es mi __tia__
   My mother's sister is my aunt.
8. La hermana de mi tío es mi __madre__
   My aunt's sister is my mother.

110

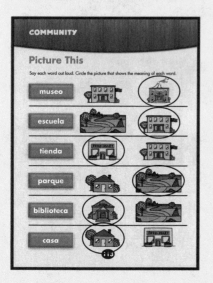

COMMUNITY

Picture This

Say each word out loud. Circle the picture that shows the meaning of each word.

museo
escuela
tienda
parque
biblioteca
casa

113

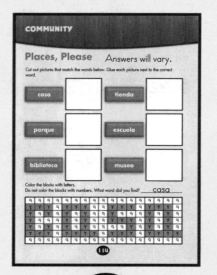

COMMUNITY

Places, Please — Answers will vary.

Cut out pictures that match the words below. Glue each picture next to the correct word.

casa | tienda
parque | escuela
biblioteca | museo

Color the blocks with letters.
Do not color the blocks with numbers. What word did you find? __casa__

114

COMMUNITY

Places to Go

Say each word out loud. Copy each word and color the picture.

museo — museo
escuela — escuela
casa — casa
tienda — tienda
biblioteca — biblioteca
parque — parque

115

ANSWER KEY

Where Am I?

Refer to the word bank and write the Spanish word for each place in the community pictured.

escuela	granja	biblioteca	tienda
museo	casa	apartamento	zoológico
iglesia	restaurante	cine	parque

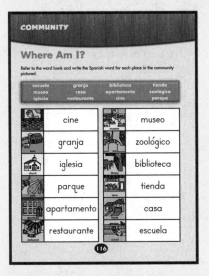

	cine		museo
	granja		zoológico
	iglesia		biblioteca
	parque		tienda
	apartamento		casa
	restaurante		escuela

116

Around the House

Copy the Spanish words. Then, write the English words below them.

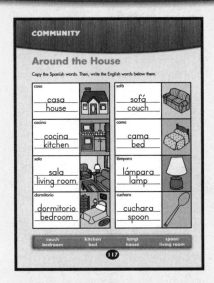

casa
casa
house

sofá
sofá
couch

cocina
cocina
kitchen

cama
cama
bed

sala
sala
living room

lámpara
lámpara
lamp

dormitorio
dormitorio
bedroom

cuchara
cuchara
spoon

| couch | kitchen | lamp | spoon |
| bedroom | bed | house | living room |

117

Around the Block

Write the Spanish words from the word bank that fit in these word blocks. Write the English below the blocks.

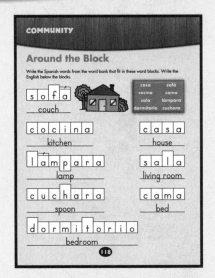

casa	sofá
cocina	cama
sala	lámpara
dormitorio	cuchara

s o f á
couch

c o c i n a
kitchen

c a s a
house

l á m p a r a
lamp

s a l a
living room

c u c h a r a
spoon

c a m a
bed

d o r m i t o r i o
bedroom

118

A Blue House

Copy the sentences in Spanish on the first lines. Write the sentences in English on the second lines.

1. La casa es azul. La casa es azul.
   The house is blue.
2. La sala es café. La sala es café.
   The living room is brown.
3. El dormitorio es morado. El dormitorio es morado.
   The bedroom is purple.
4. La cuchara es verde. La cuchara es verde.
   The spoon is green.
5. El sofá es rosado. El sofá es rosado.
   The sofa is pink.
6. La cama es azul. La cama es azul.
   The bed is blue.
7. La lámpara es amarilla. La lámpara es amarilla.
   The lamp is yellow.

Challenge:
La fruta está en la cocina. La fruta está en la cocina.
The fruit is in the kitchen.

119

Home, Sweet Home

At the bottom of each picture, copy the Spanish word.

dormitorio vaso cocina casa
sala baño toalla cama
estufa televisión lámpara teléfono

Write the Spanish word after each room or household item.

bathroom	baño	lamp	lámpara
towel	toalla	bed	cama
television	televisión	telephone	teléfono
bedroom	dormitorio	stove	estufa
living room	sala	glass	vaso
kitchen	cucina	house	casa

120

Draw and Color Your Classroom

Draw and color a picture for each word listed. Which ones do you have in your classroom? Circle them. **Answers will vary.**

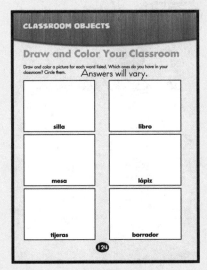

silla	libro
mesa	lápiz
tijeras	borrador

124

Classroom Things

Copy each word and color the picture.

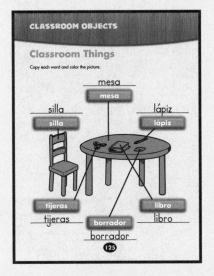

mesa
mesa
silla
silla
lápiz
lápiz
tijeras
tijeras
libro
libro
borrador
borrador

125

New Classroom Words

Say each word out loud. Copy each word and color the picture.

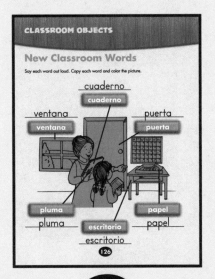

cuaderno
cuaderno
ventana
ventana
puerta
puerta
pluma
pluma
escritorio
escritorio
papel
papel

126

Listen Carefully

Say each word out loud. Circle the picture that tells the meaning of each word.

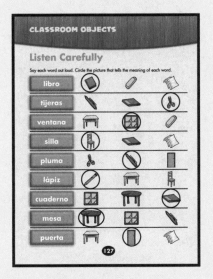

| libro |
| tijeras |
| ventana |
| silla |
| pluma |
| lápiz |
| cuaderno |
| mesa |
| puerta |

127

255

CLASSROOM OBJECTS

Show and Tell

Write the Spanish for each clue in the crossword puzzle.

ACROSS
1. notebook
5. scissors
7. pen
8. eraser
10. pencil
11. table
12. chair

DOWN
2. desk
3. window
4. book
6. door
9. paper

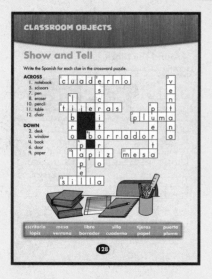

Crossword answers: cuaderno, ven(tana), tijeras, pluma, borrador, lapiz, mesa, silla

escritorio · mesa · libro · silla · tijeras · puerta
lápiz · ventana · borrador · cuaderno · papel · pluma

128

CLASSROOM OBJECTS

Pencil and Paper

Copy the following sentences in Spanish. Then, write the English meanings.

1. El libro es rojo. El libro es rojo.
   The book is red.
2. La silla es café. La silla es café.
   The chair is brown.
3. El cuaderno es morado. El cuaderno es morado.
   The notebook is purple.
4. La mesa es verde. La mesa es verde.
   The table is green.
5. El lápiz es rosado. El lápiz es rosado.
   The pencil is pink.
6. El borrador es amarillo. El borrador es amarillo.
   The eraser is yellow.
7. La ventana es azul. La ventana es azul.
   The window is blue.
8. El escritorio es anaranjado. El escritorio es anaranjado.
   The desk is orange.
9. El papel es blanco. El papel es blanco.
   The paper is white.

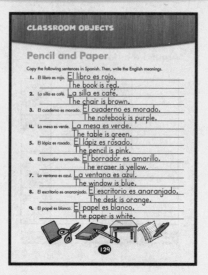

129

CLASSROOM OBJECTS

Around the Room

In each box, copy the Spanish word for the classroom object pictured.

silla		mesa	
silla		mesa	
puerta		pluma	
puerta		pluma	
ventana		borrador	
ventana		borrador	
lápiz		cuaderno	
lápiz		cuaderno	
papel		libro	
papel		libro	
escritorio		tijeras	
escritorio		tijeras	

Write the Spanish words from above next to the English words.

window **ventana**   chair **silla**   table **mesa**
eraser **borrador**   scissors **tijeras**   door **puerta**
desk **escritorio**   pen **pluma**   notebook **cuaderno**
paper **papel**   book **libro**   pencil **lápiz**

130

CLASSROOM OBJECTS

A Fitting Design

Write the Spanish words from the word bank that fit in these word blocks. Write the English meanings below the blocks.

ventana · silla · pluma · mesa · cuaderno
papel · tijeras · libro · puerta · lápiz

silla
chair

mesa
table

papel
paper

lápiz
pencil

cuaderno
notebook

libro
book

pluma
pen

tijeras
scissors

ventana
window

puerta
door

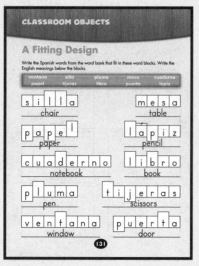

131

CLASSROOM OBJECTS

Where's My Pencil?

Circle the Spanish words that you find in the word search. Then, write the English meaning of each word. Words can be across, down, diagonal, or backward.

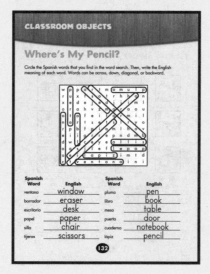

Spanish Word	English	Spanish Word	English
ventana	window	pluma	pen
borrador	eraser	libro	book
escritorio	desk	mesa	table
papel	paper	puerta	door
silla	chair	cuaderno	notebook
tijeras	scissors	lápiz	pencil

132

CLASSROOM OBJECTS

Classroom Clutter   Answers will vary.

Draw a picture to illustrate each of the Spanish words. Refer to the word bank at the bottom of the page to help you.

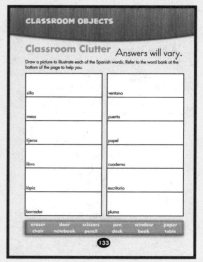

silla	ventana
mesa	puerta
tijeras	papel
libro	cuaderno
lápiz	escritorio
borrador	pluma

eraser · door · scissors · pen · window · paper
chair · notebook · pencil · desk · book · table

133